Many thanks to my colleagues and friends Bas and Rene whose detailed comments really helped me improve this book.

Many thanks to my wonderful wife for the time spent reading those pages, asking relevant questions and helping me to clarify my convoluted style.

*Progress is impossible
without change, and those
who cannot change their
minds cannot change
anything.*

*George Bernard
Shaw*

INTRODUCTION

Before delving into what this book proposes, let's focus on what it will not provide. This is not a change management book and it will not make you a change management expert. There are very good change management books already published and the world may not need another one. In addition, you can only become an expert at something by experience, mistakes, and daily improvement. This is not an Agile book either. The subject of Agile is also covered in multiple in-depth books.

So, what is the purpose of this book? I propose to analyze the impact of Agile methodologies on change management activities. Change management is one of the key success factors of any project. It helps embed change inside and outside an organization in order to achieve the objectives stated by the project. Change management helps sustain the use of a new IT system, the use of a new manufacturing process inside a plant or the acceptance of a new law by a community.

A vast majority of large projects are using some kind of waterfall methodology. It means large batches of sequential project works that have their counterparts in several aspects of a change management model. After your product development, for example, you will provide the almost final solution to a group of end-users to have some impact assessment activities. The development may have lasted more than several months and for a large organization, the impact assessment is sometimes organized in large workshops around the globe to ensure that all local idiosyncrasies are covered (which may take another 2 to 3 months). In Agile, months turn into weeks and weeks into days. How do you make it happen, when a project runs on sprints that last 2 to 4 weeks and can deliver increments of product every 2 to 3 months (or in some cases on a daily basis)?

This book will try to answer that question. As Agile frameworks are still unfolding, there may be multiple updates before we can arrive at a stable environment (in the same manner it took 2 decades before a stable and widespread use of the Lean Manufacturing model). It will be organized in 2 parts: The first one (Chapter 1, 2 and 3) will be about Agile and its different schools with a more detailed run at the Scrum framework. Chapter 3 to 5 will give an overview of change management with a more detailed view of one real-life model used in a large transitional company. The final block will propose and review a new Agile model dedicated to Agile development framework while integrating change led by the design Thinking methodologies.

PART 1: CLARIFICATION AND LANDSCAPE

CHAPTER 1: WHAT IS AGILE?

AGILE ORIGIN STORY

Agile started in 2001 in Utah where 17 senior developers, fed up by the failure of the waterfall approach, met and shared their experience. They were focused on bringing lightweight methodologies in the IT development world. They had all experimented and tinkered with those principles in their organizations. They also brought into the mix empirical method (also known as scientific method). For those who have experiences in lean manufacturing, they came up with a philosophy extremely similar but applied to IT product development. Since then, it has been extended to general product development. Let's quickly browse the principles that they were trying to bring down. Then we can do some myth busting.

WATERFALL MODEL

Before waterfall, there was no specific IT project methodology applied. Waterfall was the replication of standard engineering practices to the new IT world. It is a sequential process where when one step is completed you can move to the next. In large engineering projects (like plane manufacturing or construction), any downstream change is extremely costly. Therefore, you try to lock everything in before you move to the next stage of a project. It started in the 50's and was becoming prevalent in the 70's. In 1976, the term waterfall was coined. As a crown achievement, the Pentagon adopted the waterfall approach in 1985. In the original waterfall model, we have the phases described below:

1. Requirements: captured in a product requirements document

2. Analysis: resulting in models, schema, and business rules

3. Design: resulting in the software architecture

4. Coding: the development, proving, and integration of software

5. Testing: the systematic discovery and debugging of defects

6. Operations: the installation, migration, support, and maintenance of complete systems

All subsequent models are a variation of that original one. If we look at it through an Agile lens, the 2 main characteristics of the waterfall are:

• You cannot move to the next phase without having fully completed the previous one.

• Everything must be documented to avoid any uncertainty and any downstream issue.

AGILE MYTHS

Before precisely describing the concept of Agile development, let's focus on some prevalent myths on this topic.

MYTH #1: AGILE IS A METHODOLOGY

That is the most prevalent myth and the main reason why some companies are disappointed with Agile. Agile is a set of values and principles that can be summed as 4 values described in the Agile Manifesto and the 12 guiding principles that were created during the Utah meeting. It's nothing more, nothing less. The 4 values are described as follows:

"We are uncovering better ways of developing software by doing it and helping others do it. Through this work we have come to value:

1. Individuals and interactions over processes and tools

2. Working software over comprehensive documentation

3. Customer collaboration over contract negotiation

4. Responding to change over following a plan

That is, while there is value in the items on the right, we value the items on the left more."

There are several important things stated in those values. The first one is that the constant change in Agile methodology is based on continuous improvement. We can see that in the use of the progressive tense and the word "uncovering". It also means that the discovery is not complete yet. The second point is its focus on working software development even though those principles are used currently by non-IT companies. The last piece is that it's an experimental framework. The part of the sentence "Through this work, we have come" shows a dedication to the scientific or empirical method and not a pure academic thought process.

Those values are complemented by 12 principles that guide the people working in an Agile environment:

1. The highest priority is to satisfy the customer through early and continuous delivery of valuable software.

2. Welcome changing requirements, even late in development. Agile processes harness change for the customer's competitive advantage.

3. Deliver working software frequently, from a couple of weeks to a couple of months, with a preference to the shorter timescale.

4. Business people and developers must work together daily throughout the project.

5. Build projects around motivated individuals. Give them the environment and the support they need, and trust them to get the job done.

6. The most efficient and effective method of conveying information to and within a Development Team is face-to-face conversation.

7. Working software is the primary measure of progress.

8. Agile processes promote sustainable development. The sponsors, developers, and users should be able to maintain a constant pace indefinitely.

9. Continuous attention to technical excellence and good design enhances agility.

10. Simplicity — the art of maximizing the amount of work not done — is essential.

11. The best architectures, requirements, and designs emerge from self-organizing teams.

12. At regular intervals, the team reflects on how to become more effective and then tunes and adjusts its behavior accordingly.

Myth #2: There is only one Agile

This is a direct consequence of the previous myth. If Agile is not a methodology, then different people created different frameworks that suit their needs. The most famous is Scrum but you have also Extreme Programming, Kanban, Lean programming; SAFe, LeSS... We will see the commonalities and differences in the subsequent paragraphs. So, if a company is telling you "we are moving to Agile" without more details, you can safely assume that they believe some version of the above myths.

AGILE KEY CONCEPTS

Regardless of the Agile framework you are using, they are several key common components to all of them. They are the foundation of Agile. For those who come from a lean manufacturing background, the sound of Agile concepts will be extremely familiar as it's focused on transparency, small batches, backlog control (with cards that look like Kanban), quality and self-governing team. Let's review a quick glossary of the key Agile concept:

o **User story:** User stories are all the features that the customers will need to use the product. Those user stories can be based on usability ("In need to update a price") or technical ("Connect to legacy system XXX using standard ESB system"). They are composed of 3 parts: Customer, functionality, and benefit. They are stored and prioritized in the product backlog.

o **Product backlog:** This is the repository of all the user stories (features) and the backbone of the method. It is owned by the Product Owner (see Scrum below). This backlog is reprioritized after each sprint and is constantly updated based on customer or internal users' requirements.

o **Sprint:** The sprint is a time-boxed increment of 2-4 weeks where the Development Team is developing features described in the user stories. At the start of it, you plan it with the Product Owner. During the sprint, the Development Team will design, code and test them. At the end, you have a sprint review, which is a meeting where you present the product to the stakeholders. A product delivery is generally composed of several sprints where customers' and stakeholders' feedbacks are integrated into the product backlog. The lean manufacturing analogy of a sprint would be takt time and small batch size.

o **Daily meetings:** In any Agile methodology, you will have daily meetings (no more than 15 min) that give everyone the status of their work. The purpose is to ensure collaboration among team members so that anyone can help removing impediments for the team. The topic covered by each member would be: I completed XXX, I'm now working on YYY and I have an issue with ZZZ.

o **Measurement and visibility:** Transparency is a major concept in Agile. Everything everyone does is visible. The Product Owner work is visible through the product backlog, the effectiveness of the sprint is visible on the sprint board, the Product Backlog burn down chart and the release chart.

THINKING OF AGILE: THE WRONG PATH

Many companies decide to move to Agile without an understanding of what it really means: a complete reshaping of the leadership belief of a company. After several years in the field and many discussions with colleagues and peers, I saw the same pattern unfold several times. In a large transnational company, a few large projects failed using the waterfall approach leading to delay, project closure and loss of faith. Executives still understand the need for change and realize that they need to speed up their transformation. During an executive event, somebody makes the statement that:" we need to become more Agile" (who wants to be less Agile anyway?). A few rounds of formal and informal discussions later, the statement becomes: "We need to become Agile". Note that the word "more" had been dropped and the meaning of the sentence is shifting. We may have some executives who read about Agile interjecting:" we need Product Owners". The next thing you know, the company is embarking on an organizational change either by themselves which may lead to nothing or with the help of consultants without genuine experience on the topic (how many consultants have been Scrum Masters or Product Owners) which may lead to something slightly better but will cost much, much more. The purpose of the following chapter is to clarify a little more what Agile is, what it can deliver and how it can deliver it. As such, we may have a better idea of what Agile really entails.

CHAPTER 2: AGILE FRAMEWORKS

As we saw in the previous chapter, Agile is a general term covering various approaches that started in software development. There is no single Agile framework out there but several. We can sort them into 3 broad categories illustrated in the image below:

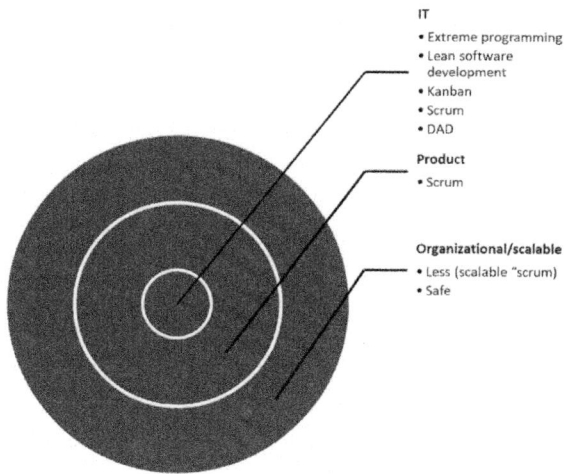

IT
• Extreme programming
• Lean software development
• Kanban
• Scrum
• DAD

Product
• Scrum

Organizational/scalable
• Less (scalable "scrum)
• Safe

The first category is composed of systems dedicated to software products development. The second one is focused on frameworks that outgrew the software industry to work in any kind of product development. The last one is catering to the problem of Agile scalability i.e. the ability to manage complex product development that requires several teams that may not even be collocated. This list is not exhaustive but covers the most used. There are other models like Feature-Driven Development (FDD), Agile Modeling (AM), to name a few. They all look relatively similar in their approach and as such, it would not be value added (remember that Agile place a strong emphasis on value) to go over through all of them.

IT FOCUSED SYSTEMS

EXTREME PROGRAMMING

XP is one of the most used Agile frameworks in IT development. It could be described as:" Scrum under amphetamine". It's an extremely disciplined model focused on delivering software quickly, continuously and at high-quality. Its key characteristics are: customer involvement, rapid feedback loops, continuous testing, continuous planning. Excellent teamwork is required to deliver working software every 1-3 weeks. XP is based on 5 values (simplicity, communication, feedback, respect, and courage) and twelve supporting practices (very similar to the Agile manifesto):

- Planning Game

- Small Releases

- Customer Acceptance Tests

- Simple Design

- Pair Programming

- Test-Driven Development

- Refactoring

- Continuous Integration

- Collective Code Ownership

- Coding Standards

- Metaphor

- Sustainable Pace

In that framework, the customer interacts closely and directly with the Development Team. Together they define and prioritize functionalities ("User Stories"). The Development Team creates the estimates, plans the work, and delivers the highest priority user stories. The delivery is a working, tested software.

LEAN SOFTWARE DEVELOPMENT

Lean Software Development is inspired by the principles of the Lean enterprise started as Lean manufacturing by Toyota. Lean Software Development focuses on delivering Value to the customer and efficiency of the development process. The principles of Lean Software Development are:

• Eliminating Waste

• Amplifying Learning

• Deciding as Late as Possible

• Delivering as Fast as Possible

• Empowering the Team

• Building Integrity In

• Seeing the Whole

As we can see, the principles look similar to the ones Scrum uses (see below for details on Scrum). This will be a common thread of all the Agile methodologies. Lean methodology focuses on waste elimination through valuable features selection, selection prioritization, and batch reduction. The other main objective is to rely on rapid feedback and customer involvement. Lean uses the notion of "pull" where a specific user story would be pulled by the customers to define the priorities. Like in any other Agile framework, it relies on a decision-making authority at small teams' level (or even individuals). It also concentrates the team effectiveness, ensuring that all team members are as productive as possible. The use of continuous improvement principles supports that effort.

KANBAN SOFTWARE DEVELOPMENT

The Kanban Method is used by organizations to manage the creation of products with an emphasis on continuous delivery without overburdening the

Development Team. Like Scrum, Kanban is a process designed to help teams work together more effectively. Kanban is a Lean manufacturing tool that indicates to the operator what to do next and in which quantity. This tool is used as a trigger for work, a visual management system and a WIP (Work in Progress) limitation system where you only produce the necessary quantity. Similarly, in software development, Kanban is focused on:

• Visualizing the work in real time

• Limiting the amount of work in progress

• What is coming next when something is done

The issue with Kanban framework is that it's using a lean tool in lieu and place of a methodology. In Lean Manufacturing, the real core is continuous improvement and the required people coaching for that to happen, not the tools themselves.

DISCIPLINE AGILE DELIVERY (DAD)

The official definition of DAD is the following:

"Disciplined Agile Delivery (DAD) process decision framework is a people-first, learning-oriented hybrid Agile approach to IT solution delivery. It has a risk-value delivery lifecycle, is goal-driven, is enterprise aware, and is scalable."

DAD was developed from 2006 to 2012 and is aimed to fill in the gaps in the Scrum methodology. DAD is a modified version of Scrum with add-ons borrowed from other Agile methodologies like Extreme Programming (XP), Kanban, Lean and Agile Modelling to name a few. It recreates a phased approach with the following steps: Inception, Construction, and Transition. It also requires having an Architecture Owner as a part of the team. DAD is a strong methodology with a focus on design and architecture but is also perceived as vague on how to execute it properly.

Product development framework

Scrum

Scrum is an Agile product development framework. It was developed by Ken Schwaber, Mike Beedle, and Jeff Sutherland among others and is still evolving today. Scrum is the most known (and used) Agile framework. We can link its success to its focus on simplicity, productivity, and ability to integrate parts of other Agile methodologies.

Scrum is composed of 3 roles: The Product Owner, the Scrum Master, and the Development Team. The Product Owner fully owns the product developed. He or she works with customers and internal stakeholders to define the functionalities of the product. He or she works then with the Development Team, the Scrum Team, as well as the various stakeholders and prioritizes "user stories" (system features) in a "Product Backlog". The Development Team then estimates each feature in term of workload and delivers them at the end of each sprint. The Development is a self-governed team that is free to operate in the way it wants inside the Scrum framework. The best analogy would be a military commando that would have all freedom to operate as long as it respects the rules of engagement. In that trinity, the Scrum Master is the last role. He or She is not a Project Manager or a Team leader. He or she is the remover of obstacles for the project and the Agile coach of the Development team. Scrum theory is extremely simple, but its application requires focus and discipline. We will develop those notions in detail in the next chapter as it will be the foundation of our Agile model definition in the last part.

SCALABLE SYSTEMS

LARGE SCALE SCRUM (LESS)

LeSS was created in 2005 to help large organizations implement Scrum in their organizations. Its purpose is to be scalable and adaptable to any company of any size at any level. LeSS is composed of 2 sub-frameworks.

The first framework is targeted toward smaller companies up to 10 Scrum Teams. The second is focused on larger companies where hundreds of people (in a dozen of Scrum) can work on a single product. The first framework is the classical Scrum with an additional layer of coordination between the Scrum Teams. This new layer also abides by the Scrum principles (to keep the flexibility) with a "Scrum of Scrums". However, you keep a single Product Owner. The second Framework (a.k.a. LeSS Huge) creates the role of APOs (Area POs) to scale the model. The best example of the use of LeSS is coming from BMW which is starting a transition towards that methodology for the iCar direct-sales process.

SCALES AGILE FRAMEWORK (SAFE)

SAFe stands for "Scaled Agile Framework" and is the most known scaled Agile framework currently in the market. Its purpose is to move a company from a non-Agile to an Agile execution. Its main strength lies in its highly prescriptive structure. Despite some success in implementation in large companies (Intel, Fannie Mae or Vodafone), some in the Agile community criticize SAFe for lacking dedication to the Agile values. They argue that it misses the transformational values of Agile and just add an incremental Agile varnish on an existing hierarchical structure. It does not put the ownership of decision at the right level and keeps some managerial decision-making processes. This framework creates various structures to ensure scalability: Team level, Program level, and Portfolio level. At the team level, it can use any Agile methodology (Scrum, Kanban…). At Program level, it creates the notion of an Agile Release Train that links the teams together. At Portfolio level, it aligns the Trains with the strategic goals of the company. If we had to sum it up in a simplistic manner we could tag it as "Scrum mixed up with some PMO and Portfolio management practices".

DELIVERY IN AGILE

This is a key notion from a change management standpoint. Indeed, how you release your product will impact the change activities that you will have to manage. However, the word "release" needs to be defined first. Depending on the type of product or software you are working on, releases can be organized in 3 manners:

Always-on release: This is mainly for smaller applications or for companies with very advanced and flexible technological landscape. It means that you are delivering something new to the customer as soon as it is ready. This type of release can only be done for the most mature Agile companies.

Sprint release: You release your shippable product at the end of the sprint when the Product Owner officially accepts it. As you a releasing something new every 2-4 weeks, this type of release also requires a strong Agile leadership and technical maturity.

Release Backlog: This is not an official Agile term but as we have a Product Backlog, a Sprint Backlog, the concept of Release Backlog is easily understandable. In companies working with a web of older systems or critical software, an "always-on" release schedule is unrealistic (even if it should be considered as the end goal) and maybe even dangerous. Consequently, the existing deployment cycle is generally relatively long to include testing, architecture roll out... As such, the increments are aggregated in a block that will be shipped to the customer every pre-defined timeframe (around 3-12 months). This is the approach that we will consider from now on in this book. Indeed, if your company is moving toward an Agile approach, it means that your technical and leadership landscape is not mature yet. Therefore, you are most likely to use that type of release strategy.

CONCLUSION

All Agile frameworks are similar in their approach and focus. We can group them into 3 categories: those dedicated to software work, those transferable to development of any type of product and the few that can be scaled at company level. We can visualize again that in the graph below:

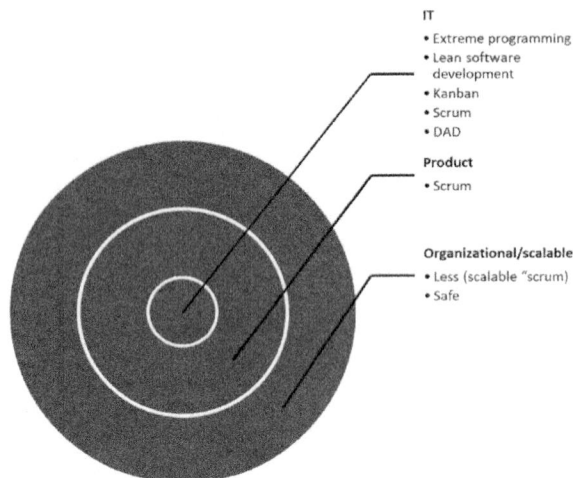

IT
• Extreme programming
• Lean software development
• Kanban
• Scrum
• DAD

Product
• Scrum

Organizational/scalable
• Less (scalable "scrum)
• Safe

In the next chapter, we will delve into Scrum for two reasons. First, it is the most currently used framework in the business environment. In addition, as it's not dedicated to the world of software, a large majority of product development and change management activities associated will be covered in the next chapter.

CHAPTER 3: HOW SCRUM WORKS

Now that we have reviewed the different frameworks, let's focus one of them: Scrum. This framework was chosen because it is one of the most used inside and outside IT and it is also at the core of the organizational models like LeSS and SAFe. We will first have a list of operational terms used in Scrum. We will then describe the roles in a Scrum Team. It is extremely important as Scrum is a people-oriented model. It means that it can only work if each role is executed properly. We will then define the Scrum key concepts and we will finally review how a product development is managed.

SCRUM GLOSSARY

To fully understand how Scrum works, we need to understand first the vocabulary used by the Scrum guidelines. This is basic glossary; the exhaustive one is provided in the addendum of the book.

Sprint: A time-boxed effort where no change can happen in the scope (maintained in the Sprint backlog). The sprint length is generally fixed for the entire project and cannot be less than 2 weeks and last more than 4 weeks.

Sprint Backlog: Backlog of all the user stories that need to be developed by the Development Team during a Sprint. During that phase, the Development Team is free to finish the stories in the way they decide is the most effective. The backlog will be updated daily accordingly.

Product Backlog: List of all the user stories (product features or requirements) that are required by the customers. This backlog is prioritized by user stories value (generally estimated in ROI if possible). It is constantly reprioritized based on what has been delivered by the Development Team in each sprint, what customer are giving in term of feedback, what the company wants as an outcome and how the technology is evolving.

Shippable Product: This is the outcome of a sprint. The exact definition is a product that is fully ready but has not yet been delivered to the customer.

Estimation: This is the method used by the team to assess the risk, complexity, and effort required to produce a user story. It can be expressed in hours or with a points system. Those estimations are used by the team to ensure that they have the right amount of work during the sprint. For example, if they can produce generally 50 points worth of user stories, they can only have 50 points in their sprint backlog.

Team Velocity: It defines the workload (generally in points) that the team can produce during a sprint. At the end of each sprint during a meeting called "Sprint Retrospective", the Scrum Master will use continuous improvement and coaching techniques to help the team increase its velocity.

Release chart: This is the chart updated at the end of each sprint to measure the progress of the product development. There are 2 types of charts that can be used: burn up or burn down. The burn up chart adds the number of points done during each sprint towards the total number of necessary points. The burn down is the reverse version starting with the total number of points and subtracting the results of each sprint. The team records the number of points produced during each sprint in one the following charts:

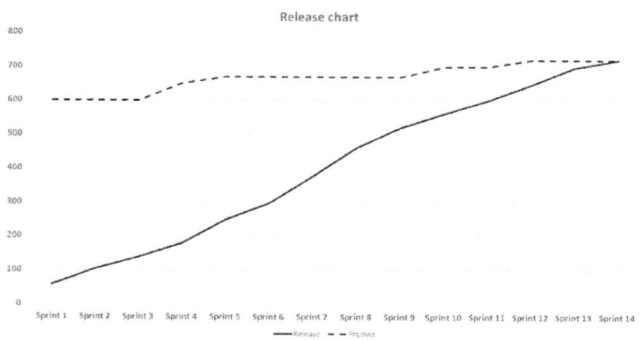

Ceremonies: Scrum call certain meetings ceremonies. The sprint planning meeting, the daily scrum, the sprint review meeting and the sprint retrospective. It emphasizes their importance in the framework. For the sake of clarity, we will still call them "meeting" in the book.

Burn down and burn up charts: Those graphs are used during the sprint to measure where the team is every day in term of point production. This graph is updated during the daily Scrum meeting. We can see an example below:

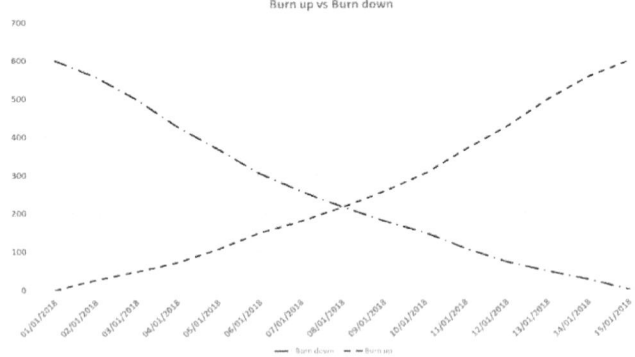

SCRUM ROLES AND RESPONSIBILITIES

There are 3 roles in Scrum: The Product Owner, the Scrum Master and the Development Team as illustrated below.

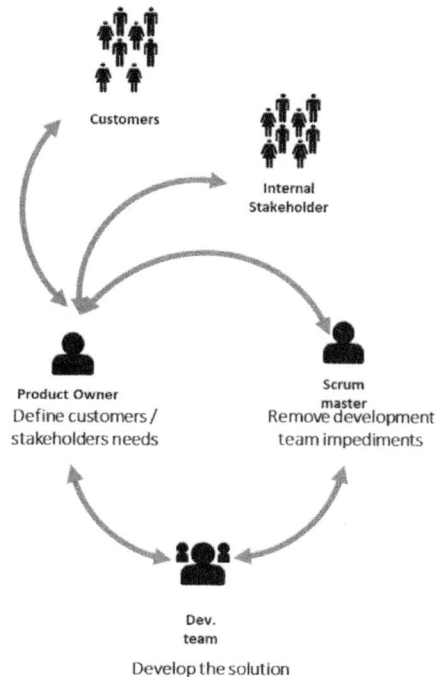

Customers

Internal
Stakeholder

Product Owner
Define customers /
stakeholders needs

Scrum
master
Remove development
team impediments

Dev.
team
Develop the solution

PRODUCT OWNER

As the name indicates, the Product Owner owns the product. But, contrary to a lot of companies that have an "owner" who does not really own anything, the Product Owner has full accountability on the direction the product takes, the features inside and the go-to-market strategy as well as budgetary concerns. It means also that he will be fully accountable if the project goes wrong. This a high reward, high exposure and high-risk position.

The Product Owner is responsible to transform an idea to a product vision, interact with customers (internal or external) of the product to translate his vision into features (user stories), prioritize those stories based on value (generally measured in ROI), work with the Development Team and the Scrum Master to prioritize user stories in each sprint, update the Product Backlog on what has really been delivered and formally accepts the product of each sprint.

In addition, during each sprint, he or she is in constant contact with the Development Team (and the Scrum Master) to see how the sprint is progressing and with customers to gather new needs for the product. He is also directly involved with senior stakeholders that have a vested interest in a product that is part of the company strategy.

As we can see, the role of a Product Owner is multi-dimensional and highly demanding as well as requires a strong business insight. It requires a large network, a strong drive, and very high communication and organizational skills. If the product is IT-based, it would also require some IT knowledge and an ability to understand the IT up-to-date technological development.

SCRUM MASTER

Let's start with what the Scrum Master is not: A Project Manager or a Team Leader. We will see in the following paragraphs that all functions of a Project Manager are unnecessary or covered by the Product Owner. In the first case, the classical function of leading the team is irrelevant because high-functioning Scrum Teams are self-managed. On the second part, the Product Owner is accountable for the progress of the development and the notion of milestones is irrelevant in a sprint mode as we will see below.

So, if the Scrum Master is none of the above roles, what function does he or she have? The Scrum guidelines sum up the role of the Scrum Master by the following words: Servant Leadership. We can translate that into 2 main functions: coach and remover. We mentioned earlier that high-functioning Scrum Teams are self-managed. However, to reach this state, coaching is necessary. This is why a Scrum Master cannot be inexperienced in the application of the Scrum framework as he is the reference and the expert. He may also have to coach the Product Owner.

The role of remover is his main other function. During the daily Scrum meeting (see below), the team states the impediments they are facing. The role of the Scrum Master is to remove them if the team cannot do it on its own. Impediments can be internal problems like missing skillset in the team. Some impediments are also external: lack of access to a necessary IT server, stakeholders barging in to try adding some new user stories… This aspect of the role is extremely difficult to describe as it may depend on the impediments that the team is facing. However, it requires a very large network inside the company and a self-effacing persona (the star of the show is the Product Owner).

DEVELOPMENT TEAM

The role of the Development Team is relatively obvious, but the Scrum framework is adding some twist to it. The role of the Development Team is to develop the product owned by the Product Owner. However, the main difference from a classical project team is the team self-governance. That does not mean that they can do whatever they want whenever they want it, but that, inside the Scrum framework, they have full ownership on the development path as long as they fulfill 2 criteria: They need to work on the development of the user stories from the Sprint Backlog and the product developed during a sprint must be a "potentially shippable product".

They are first involved in the estimation of each user stories based on complexity, risk, and effort. They are then working with the Product Owner and the Scrum Master to define the sprint backlog, which is the agreed scope of the sprint.

SCRUM CYCLE

BEFORE THE FIRST SPRINT

Before the first sprint, there will be several phases concluded by the creation of the product backlog. First, the Product Owner works with customers, future users and any other stakeholder to transform the product vision into a list of requirements of user stories. This phase is critical as those user's stories are at the heart of the system. They will tell the Development Team what to develop and help the Development Team during the estimation process. When that part is done, the Product

Owner will estimate each story for the value provided. Once that phase is done, the Development Team, the Scrum Master, and the Product Owner meet to have a Product Backlog meeting. During that meeting, each user story will be reviewed for further understanding and will be assessed (using a point system) to quantify the difficulty to develop it. They will also attach acceptance criteria to each story in order for the team to define precisely when they are done. We can illustrate that part with the following process:

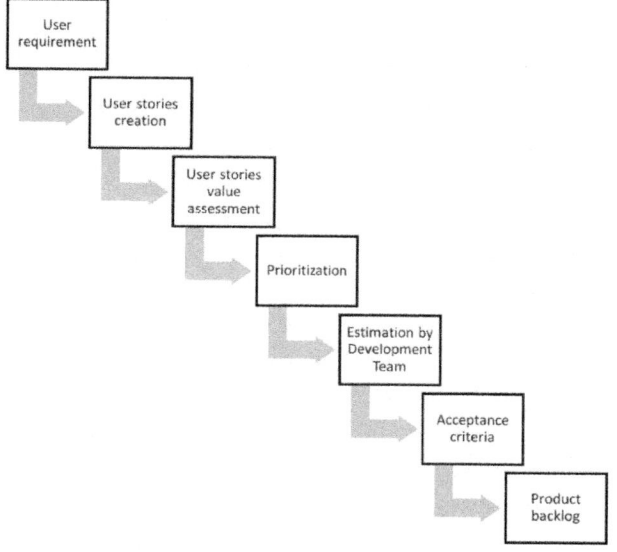

A sprint starts always with a Sprint planning meeting. During that meeting, the Scrum Team defines 2 very important things:

• **The Sprint goal:** It defines what the sprint wants to achieve. This goal needs to be put in the customer's words. For example: "I want to be able to access all my past transactions" on a merchant website.

• **The Definition of Done:** For the Sprint, the team needs to define what it means to fully complete a user's story. The idea is to ensure that there is no misalignment between team members on "what good looks like". This is often coupled with corporate guidelines on how much testing needs to be included for example.

The team will then create an aggregate of the user stories and measure the total amount of work. They will compare it to their product development speed in their previous sprints (called in Agile Velocity) to assess if the goal is realistic. If this is the first sprint, this forecast will not be accurate, and it will take at least 5 to 8 iterations to forecast more precisely what the team can achieve in a sprint. This is where an experienced Scrum Master can help ensuring that the first sprint backlogs on a new product (especially with a new team) is achievable.

During a sprint, the Development Team and the Scrum Master will meet every day to discuss for fifteen minutes. This is the Daily Scrum meeting. They will focus on 3 questions: what has been achieved? what is next? and what are the impediments? We can illustrate the sprint process with the following figure:

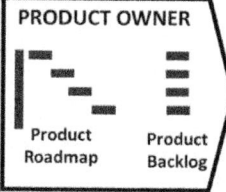
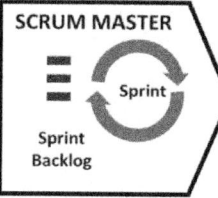

AFTER A SPRINT

At the end of the sprint, 2 extremely important meetings take place to ensure proper closure:

• **The Sprint review:** This meeting is for the team and key stakeholders as decided by the Product Owner. It takes about 4 hours for a 4 weeks sprint. The purpose is to demonstrate the product and gather feedbacks. This feedback can create new user stories that will be placed in the Product Backlog. The second outcome is the formal acceptance by the Product Owner of the minimum viable product developed by the team.

• **The Sprint retrospective:** This meeting is for the Scrum Team only. Its purpose is to assess what went well in the sprint, what could be improved and how to achieve that. The main purpose is to increases the team velocity (development speed) for the next sprints. It would last 3 to 4 hours in for a 4-week sprint. We can illustrate the flow with the following process:

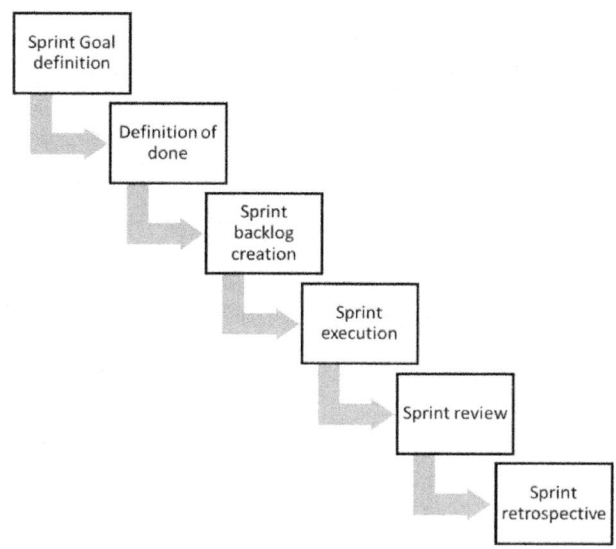

SCALABILITY: SCRUM OF SCRUM

Once you reach more than 9 people on a team, the Scrum guidelines recommend creating another Scrum Team. However, for a complex product (with teams that may not be co-located), coordination can become an issue. One technique is to create "Scrum of Scrums". Each team will appoint an "ambassador" to participate in this daily "umbrella" Scrum.

This Scrum of Scrums will have the same structure and frequency as a normal daily Scrum meeting even though it might be longer. Each ambassador will discuss the 3 topics: completion, next steps, and impediments on behalf of their teams. Impediments are focused on the issues of coordination between the teams and solutions required will have to be between teams (interface, shared responsibility....). Team impediments are solved during the team daily Scrum. This "umbrella Scrum" will have its own backlog, where items are only dedicated to improving team coordination and where they are prioritized by the Scrum of Scrum Team. More details on the topic are given in Chap. 8.

CONCLUSION

The Scrum framework (like all the other Agile frameworks) solves the issue raised by the Waterfall methodology. It is highly reactive (requirements can be added constantly in the product backlog), extremely disciplined (the scope of the Sprint Backlog does not change) and without unnecessary documentation (the Product Backlog gives a product view in real time). Based on that understanding, we can now focus on defining what is change management. We will be then equipped to see how this product development model will affect the change activities for a Change Manager.

CHAPTER 4: CHANGE MANAGEMENT

Once upon a time, a fortune 500 company wanted to change one of their old legacy sales platforms. They started a multi-year project and followed a change management model to the letter. Stakeholders were informed, high-quality training was executed on time, worldwide communication was rolled out. Before going live, decisions to postpone were based on data and prudence. The first phase of the project covering 60% of the company's business went as smooth as it could have gone for a project that size.

Then, after this success, it was time to close the gap toward 100% of the company business. Because of complacency or because it was perceived just an extension of a successful roll-out, minimal change management was executed. Just before starting, parts of the organization were not properly trained, the volume of work was underestimated, and the system suffered untested glitches. It was a 2-month hell to recover, hundreds of thousands (maybe millions) of dollars in lost revenue and a fight to regain the trust of unhappy customers. In a sense, it was a sight to behold, people fighting fires together, trying to solve customer issues and improve the system. But the fire should not have started in the first place.

In the end, the project achieved its goals, but the road could have been far smoother. In addition, despite being successful in the first phase, the only thing that people remember about this project is the second. This experience has completely stained the product. In that example (inspired by a real project), we can illustrate the difference between having proper change management and the consequence of not having it. It also illustrates, on a side note, the danger of stopping change management activities to early before the full end of a project.

WHAT IS CHANGE MANAGEMENT?

Prosci (one of the leading consulting, certification and research firm on change practices) proposes the following definition for Change management:

"Change management is the discipline that guides how we prepare, equip and support individuals to successfully adopt change in order to drive organizational success and outcomes. (…). Change management provides a structured approach for supporting the individuals in your organization to move from their own current states to their own future states."

The first part of this sentence focuses on the "what" of Change management: what it is supposed to achieve. The second part is catering for "How": How to execute it.

But why do we need it in the first place? The data gathered by Prosci over the last 8 years on more than 200 projects show that a better execution of change management leads to a better likelihood of achieving the project objectives. Data gathered by McKinsey also correlates the level of ROI with the quality of the change management in a project. As Prosci puts it:

"Change management, when applied effectively on a project, significantly increases the success rate of the effort."

However, despite its success (or because of it), change management is filled with myths or misunderstandings.

CHANGE MANAGEMENT MYTHS

In this chapter, we will browse through the most classical myths in the change management field. There are others out there and any experienced Change Manager reading those pages can add to it. But, based on my experience, I would propose that the 5 highlighted below are the most prevalent.

MYTH #1: I'M THE BOSS OR TOP-DOWN CHANGE MANAGEMENT

Every Change Manager has encountered a variation of this assumption. Senior executives in charge of large transformations (especially if they are coming from the business side) are prone to believe in their omnipotence. It may have been true fifty years ago, but it has been steadily declining and is definitively wrong with the latest generation of workers (millennials). People working in an organization nowadays require some sense of purpose that does not come with orders from higher-up. It means that people want, at the bare minimum, to understand why they need to change and, at best, to be the co-creator of that change. Therefore, top-to-bottom imposition of change on the organization will only lead to push back and the formal power of the executive will be partially or fully counter-acted by the inertia and resistance of the organization.

MYTH #2: "BUILD IT AND THEY WILL COME"

Another pervasive myth at executive level (and sometimes at IT level) is that good products sell by themselves and therefore, change management is not necessary. History is littered with wonderful products that did not sell by themselves. Being French, we made a specialty of that. Did you know that the first country in the world with e-commerce was France? At the beginning of the 80's, 15 years before Opera and Netscape, the French Telecom created a product called Minitel. It was a proprietary terminal plugged into your phone with a modem. You could buy plane tickets, chat, access information and as usual go to adult entertainment sites (nothing new under the sun). So, what happened? The French executives did not sell outside France to lock down the technology in Europe. When they tried, they assumed that as it was the only product of its kind at that time, it would sell by itself. When a better and non-proprietary technology came out (TCP/IP and internet), they were pushed out of the market. This small business example shows that the best product does not sell itself and that the role of change management is to support the "selling" inside (and sometimes outside) the organization.

MYTH #3: JUST COMMUNICATE (OR TRAIN) AND ALL WILL BE FINE

This is the next most resilient myth out there. Obviously, communication and training are necessary, but they are a mean and not the end of change management. Generally, executives (and sometimes even the project team) assume that training or sending newsletter will change the mind of the people. Mass communication channels are a highly used but demonstrably an ineffective way of moving people. How many emails are you receiving every day? How many professional social media feeds are you following? Do you really think that a mass email or newsletter will make any difference?

The same goes for training. Training can change the perception of a project but only if background works has been done before. It will help people to understand how to perform their daily tasks (the "what") but definitively not the "why". Without that part, your organization will not buy-in into the change and two main things may happen. Either they execute mindlessly their tasks and become disengaged or they will slip back to their old habits.

MYTH #4: THE PROJECT MANAGER CAN DO IT

Obviously, in any project, the Project Manager needs to know about change management. He could even have the skills to execute it for his or her project. However, it is not a matter of capabilities but a matter of time allocation. He is already busy managing milestones, ensuring IT (or engineering) delivery, managing resources both internal and external, reporting to major stakeholders and managing his or her budget. If push comes to shove (which always happens in a project), which activity will be sacrificed first? Change management! Therefore, we are going back to square one: a project without proper change management.

MYTH #5: THIS IS ONLY FOR IT PROJECT

Every project change something and needs to have that change managed. Let me give you quick example. A company wants to review its commercial offering by defining and targeting differently specific customer segments. They want to be sure that they offer what the customers want, not more, not less. A project team starts to analyze the market, working in relative secrecy. After 5 to 6 months, they come up with a full segmentation of services for those segments. They want to implement as fast as possible to ensure that those offers will be on the market early to meet their objective of revenue increase for the year. As they push for implementation, the local commercial offices start to push back: why are you changing my customer relationship, why is my customer in this segment and not in that one? The offshored service centers executing the transactional processes don't understand if and when they have to change anything in their delivery to differentiate between customers. Rapidly, the project implementation is scaled back to few segments (the least controversial) to build momentum and start delivering some elements of the project. Anything sounding familiar? This project has no IT component whatsoever, but I would strongly argue that a good Change Manager could have helped them deliver the change promised using the tools that we will review later.

CHAPTER 5: CHANGE MANAGEMENT MODELS

An brief history of change management

Once we agree that we need change management and we know what change management is not, we need to know what it's supposed to be. There are several methodologies out there that we will review. We can define several major change management frameworks currently used (including the variation in each individual companies). This list is not exhaustive and, as stated earlier, the purpose of the book is not to give an in-depth landscape of the change management field. Those models can be grouped into 2 categories. The first one is focused on a step-by-step approach, the other one, on individuals. But even the latter can be used in large organizations as companies are composed of people that may evolve at a different pace but will follow the same individual change path. In the former category, we find Beckard and Harris, GE, and Kotter. In the latter, we find ADKAR. Before reviewing them, let's go back in time to see how it all started.

The notion of change management is not new and can be traced back to the work of Taylor at the end of the

19th century. However, the notion at that time was focused on the mechanized and observable process. In the 60's, the human side of change management began to be studied and the first change management model was formalized in the 1970's (see Beckard and Harris below). In 1982, change management had its breakthrough when Julien Phillips from McKinsey published a change management model in Human Resource Management. During the next ten years, other consulting firms caught up and at the beginning of the 90's, the Big 6 consulting firms created what is now called Change Management. They integrated works from other pioneers in the field and created their own methodologies. In the 90's, change management models were widely recognized as one of the key success factors for large projects. During that decade, GE started one of the first widely used internal program called CAP (Change Acceleration program) and John Kotter published his seminal book on the topic. At the beginning of the new century, new change approach led by Prosci appeared in the change management landscape. It was more focused on the individual rather than the organizational side of change. This change of perspective will lead to the creation of the ADKAR model described in the next part.

FEW MODELS ACROSS THE YEARS

BECKARD AND HARRIS

Richard Beckhard and Rubin Harris developed their change model in 1977. It was published in "Organizational Transitions: Managing Complex Change". Their model is simple and explains that certain steps need to be accomplished for a successful change. It also uses the equation created by David Gleicher in the early 60's.

Dissatisfaction* x Vision x First steps > Resistance to change

Dissatisfaction with status quo

This formula means that the content of the first 3 parts needs to be enough to overcome the change resistance or the inertia of an organization. Beckhard and Harris identified a 7-steps to implement change.

1. Establishing a need for change

2. Building a change team

3. Create vision and values

4. Communicating and engaging

5. Empowering others

6. Noticing improvement and energizing

7. Consolidating

GE CHANGE ACCELERATION PROGRAM (CAP)

GE started a program in the 90's called "Work-Out" inspired by the Japanese quality circle. It was team-based and focused on problem-solving. Despite its success, the rate of adoption in the company was too slow for Jack Welch. He also realized that the pace of change was accelerating and that only the companies who could adapt would still be alive in few decades. Having nothing that could help accelerate change inside the company, he hired a team of consultants to find business best practices, check work in academia and come back with a ready-to-implement change toolbox that could be deployed inside GE. The change acceleration program (a.k.a. CAP) is the results of that research. CAP is a 7-step linear process relatively similar to the Beckard and Harris.

1. Leading change

2. Creating a shared need

3. Sharing a vision

4. Mobilizing commitment

5. Making change last

6. Monitoring progress

7. Changing system and structure

8-STEP KOTTER MODEL

John Paul Kotter is a Professor of Leadership at the Harvard Business School and an academic in the fields of business, leadership, and change management. Kotter's framework is one of the most used in the field of change management. It was created based on Kotter's observation of over 100 companies which had tried to reinvent themselves. His conclusion (stated in his books Leading change and Why transformation efforts fail) is that change is a process that goes through a set of steps that can be determined. In those books, he is defining 8 steps to follow:

1. Establish a sense of urgency

2. Creating a guiding coalition

3. Developing a change vision

4. Communicating the vision buy-in

5. Empowering broad-based action

6. Generating short-term win

7. Never letting up

8. Incorporating change into the culture

ADKAR

ADKAR has a slightly different take on change management as it is not a step-by-step model but a framework about changing individuals' mindsets in an organization. It was created by Jeff Hiatt after 14 years of research with change in large corporations. The ADKAR model does not revolutionize the toolkit of the Change Managers as they would have to use readiness assessments, sponsorship, communications, coaching, training and resistance management assessment. However, it ties them up at people level and not organizational level. In that model, all change activities are placed into a framework that is oriented on the phases required for an individual to change. ADKAR is an acronym with the following meaning:

- A: Awareness

- D: Desire

- K: Knowledge

- A: Ability

- R: Reinforcement

For an organization to move forward during a transformation, the Change Manager needs to respond to those 5 needs to ensure success for his or her project. Bu, this model also assumes 2 things: You have a Change Manager to help the project going through the change (so no need to create a change team) and the project sponsor is the main driver of change inside the organization.

COMMONALITIES BETWEEN MODELS

By comparing those models, we find common steps and realize that they are very similar in their approaches.

Beckhard and Harris	GE	Kotter	ADKAR
Establishing a need for change	Creating a shared need	Establish a sense of urgency	Awareness
Building a change team	Leading change	Creating a guiding coalition	Already there per model assumption
Create vision and values	Sharing a vision	Developing a change vision	Awareness
Communicating and engaging	Mobilizing commitment	Communicating the vision buy-in	Desire
			Knowledge
Empowering others		Empowering broad-based action	Ability

Noticing improvement and energizing	Monitoring progress	Generating short-term win	Reinforcement
Consolidating	Making change last	Never letting up	
	Changing system and structure	Incorporating change into culture	

CONCLUSION

In this part, we saw a description of the roles of change management and how it translated to a set of activities. We also gave an overview of the most known change models currently in the business landscape. We just need now to look at one real-life model to see how those principles are put into practice. Once done, we can focus on the impact of the Agile framework on change management.

CHAPTER 6: A REAL-LIFE MODEL

We identified key components of various known and used change models. Before we move to the core of the book, we will illustrate the application of those methodologies with a change model used in a transnational company for large transformation projects. This is an illustration and not an advocacy for that specific model but more a view on how theoretical models are applied in real life.

OVERVIEW OF THE MODEL

The overall change model can easily be illustrated by the graphic below:

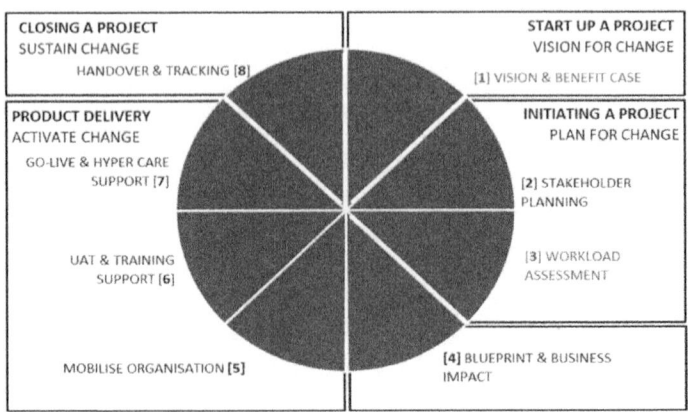

This model is largely similar to the models that we saw in the previous paragraph and come with a set of artifacts (deliverables) that support the work of the Change Managers. If we map the various linear models described above, we find the following and almost direct 1:1 link as shown below:

• **For Beckard and Harris:**

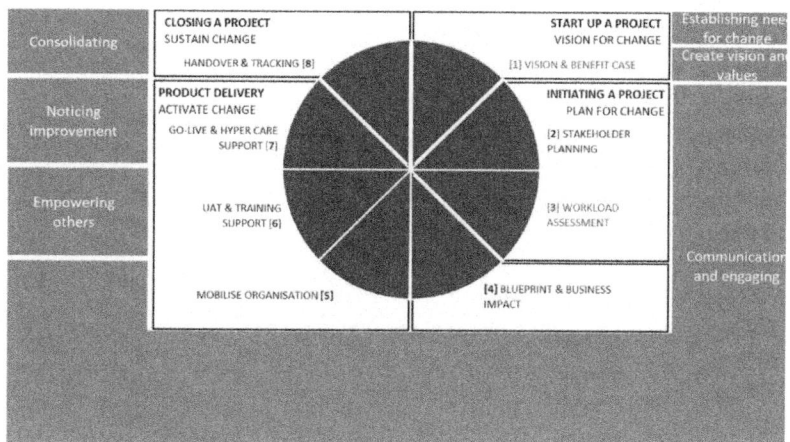

• **For the GE CAP:**

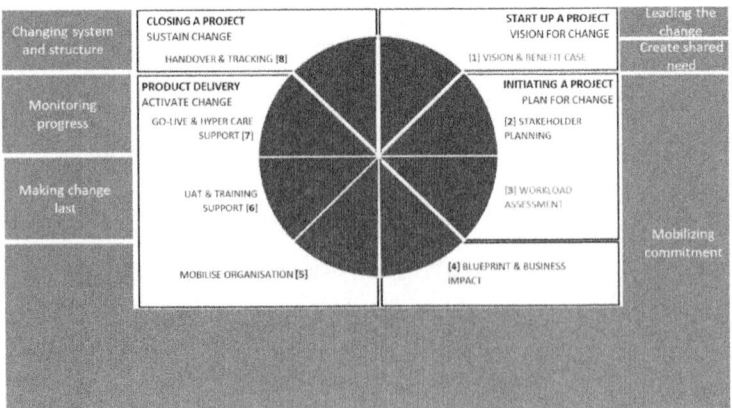

• **For Kotter:**

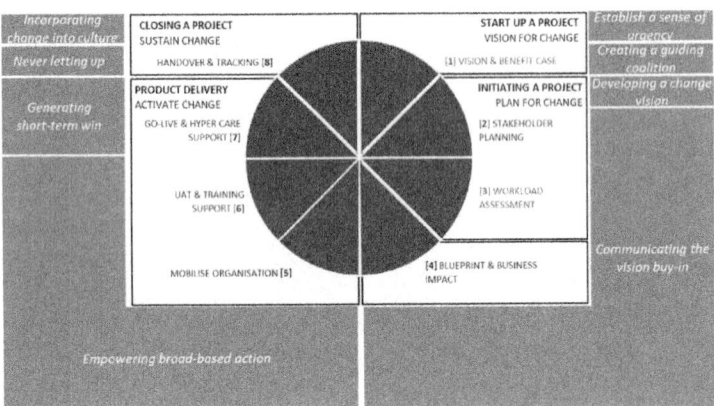

Even a non-linear model like ADKAR can be linked in the following manner:

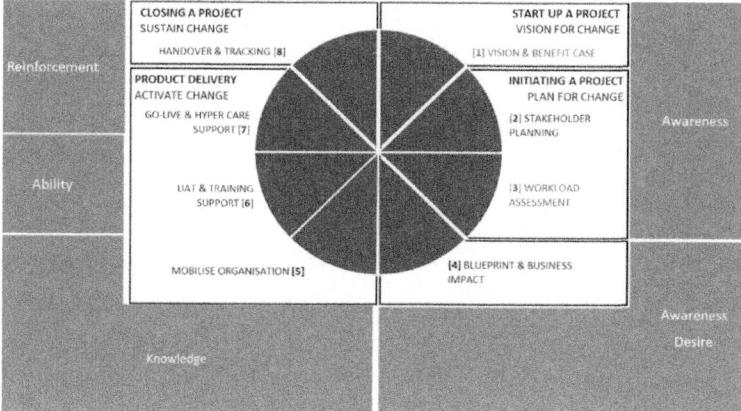

MODEL PHASES

Let's detail a little more each one of the phases of the model that we just presented.

START-UP PHASES

From a project and change standpoint, we just have an idea or a problem statement to solve. If we look at our change model, this is just the beginning of the journey. The purpose of that phase will be to validate the vision, define the expected benefits, and assess the high-level impact on the organization. At the end of the day, the purpose may also be to convince senior stakeholders to go ahead and fund the project. The tools used by the Change Managers during that phase are: the vision for change that describes the end state when the project is delivered, the benefits case highlighting all the benefits (monetary and others) and the high-level change assessment to described how the current organization will be affected. As we are going through our change journey, we will use the change wheel as an illustration. In term of change process visualization, we are at the first point of our change wheel:

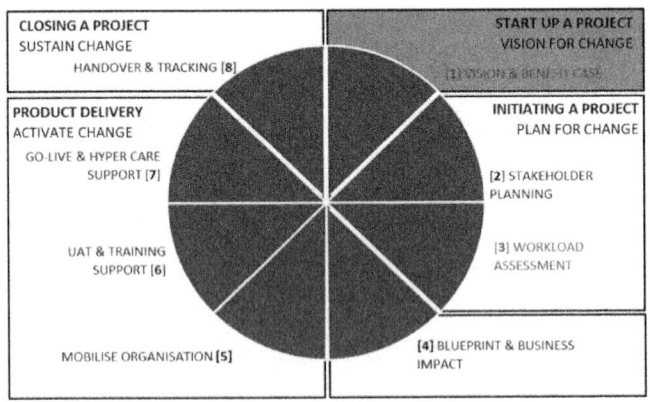

INITIATION PART 1: PLANNING

From a project management standpoint, this is when the overall project planning is created, resources allocated, and budgets are finalized for the entire project lifespan. The Project Manager will also precise and validate the project requirements. From a change management standpoint, the purpose of this phase is to understand the potential change management issues from both an organizational (organization not ready, unsuccessful past changes…) and leadership standpoint (who can drive or hinder the change). This information is a key element of the change management journey. It will drive all subsequent change actions for the project.

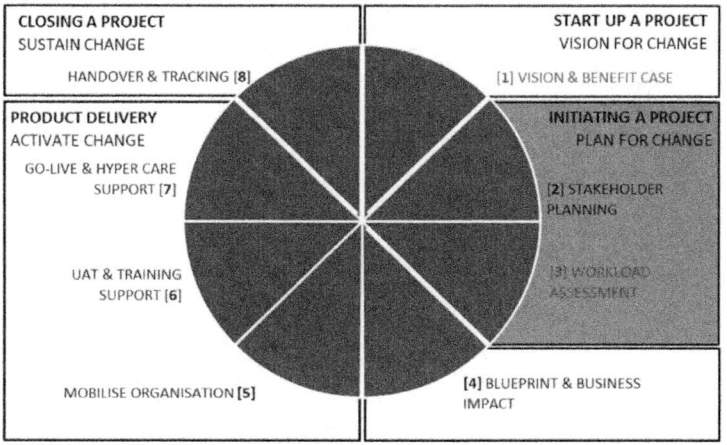

The change manager will develop a stakeholder map describing the overall list of stakeholders and their ability to impact change positively or negatively. Based on that assessment, he or she will prepare a change strategy. Finally, he or she will prepare a workload assessment to communicate with the receiving organization the expected workload and timeline. The purpose is to ensure that the organization is able to receive the expected change.

INITIATION PART 2: DEVELOPMENT AND FEEDBACK

The purpose of the phase is to develop and present the final product of the project and ensure that it corresponds to the vision stated at the early onset of the project. It can be executed in 2 ways: We can gather a reference group that will assess the solution development and will be the sounding board of the business. Another option is to organize a full road trip in the organization to present the solution, gather feedback and assess potential gaps. Depending on the size of the project and the expected impact on the organization, the Change Manager can favor one option versus the other.

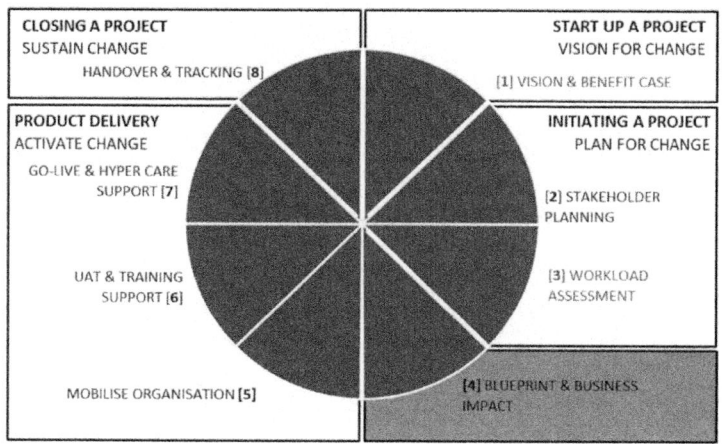

PRODUCT DELIVERY

This phase is the bulk of the Change Manager works. It moves the product from the IT world to the business organization. It has 3 main components that can be executed in parallel: organizational engagement, training, and UAT and Go-Live as seen in the change wheel:

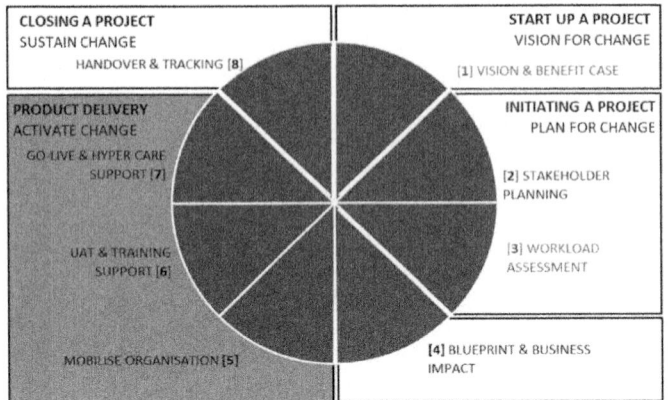

CLOSING A PROJECT
SUSTAIN CHANGE
HANDOVER & TRACKING [8]

START UP A PROJECT
VISION FOR CHANGE
[1] VISION & BENEFIT CASE

PRODUCT DELIVERY
ACTIVATE CHANGE
GO-LIVE & HYPER CARE SUPPORT [7]

INITIATING A PROJECT
PLAN FOR CHANGE
[2] STAKEHOLDER PLANNING

UAT & TRAINING SUPPORT [6]

[3] WORKLOAD ASSESSMENT

MOBILISE ORGANISATION [5]

[4] BLUEPRINT & BUSINESS IMPACT

CLOSURE

The closure part is the time where the project is done, and the product is handed over to the business. In addition, this is when you start measuring the benefit using the benefits pan and tracking defined at the onset of the project. The role of the Change Manager is to oversee the transition on both sides. On the handover, he or she will work with the standing organization to ensure that all documents are stored properly, and that staff is using the new product in a "business as usual" settings. On the benefits part, he or she will ensure that the measurements are taken according to the plan and that the reporting of the benefit execution is done to senior stakeholder and the organization at-large. This is the last part of our change wheel as seen below:

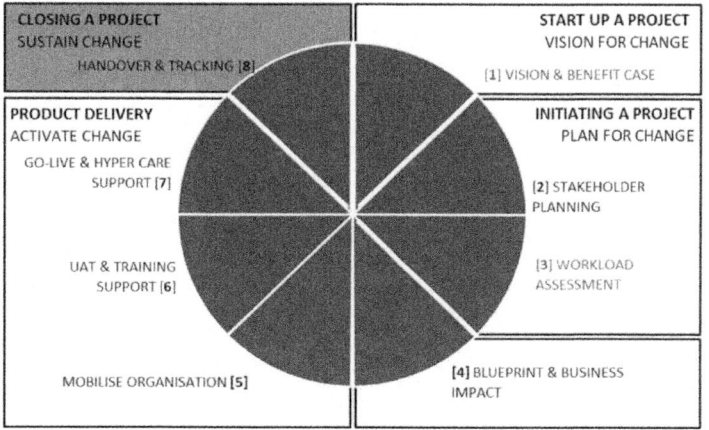

Conclusion

We are now ready to detail how Agile framework will impact the role of a Change Manager. In this part, we wanted to ensure that all readers would have at least some knowledge of both sides of the equation. To achieve that purpose, we first described what Agile was and then turned our attention to change management. Now that the introductions are done, let's get started.

PART 2: CHANGE MANAGEMENT IN AGILE

CHAPTER 7: FOR A NEW MODEL

As we have seen in the first part, Agile is changing speed, ownership and development steps of a product. Any change Manager will need to adapt to that new environment. To assess the impact on change management, we will propose a new management framework and pass it through an Agile "mixer". However, it does not mean that all the questions will be fully answered in a stable manner. As we saw earlier, Agile is a moving animal and as such answers may look different in few years. As a side note, the following paragraphs are not the only "true" way to design an Agile Change Model. But by asking the questions below, you may be able to find your own solutions. In this chapter will stay at the product and project levels. We will not delve yet into the world of the scalable model that tries to develop highly complex product requiring multiple teams. That will be the optic for chapter 8. Finally, in term of Agile framework, we will choose Scrum as it is the most used framework and can work inside and outside the IT world, but your company may use another Agile methodology.

The current issue with existing models is that they assume two things. First, the work is described in sequences. Even ADKAR works in a sequential manner to promote individual change. The second assumption is that projects have a beginning and an end. As Agile works on product and not project, it means that the notion of beginning exists, but the end may not (at least until the product has customers and funding). In addition, we are moving from a slow and sequential path to a fast and iterative path. Therefore, I would propose that we move to a different model that we will describe set-by-step in this chapter.

METHODOLOGY

For this analysis, we will propose a four-parts review in order to describe how it would look like in Scrum framework. First, we will describe each phase. We will then look at the Scrum team during that phase. Finally, we will focus on the new role of the Change Manager.

In this last section, we will ask 3 questions to ensure that we are covering all aspects:

• Question #1: What is the role the Change Manager during that phase?

• Question #2: What are the Scrum meetings the Change Manager should attend?

• Question #3: What is the impact on the Changer manager artifacts?

Is the Change Manager part of the scrum team?

Before we move forward, we need to settle a point about the position of the Change Manager. For its talk about change, Scrum is heavily focused on the development part. The notion of change management is not very developed and mainly assumed to be done by the Product Owner while talking with key stakeholders. This is the same assumption in the waterfall model where the Project Manager oversees change management. That does not mean that they don't know how to execute the related tasks, but they definitely do not have the time if they are focused on their core responsibility. In Scrum, the role of Product Owner is extremely heavy both on responsibility and time commitment. If the Product Owner fails, the product fails. Therefore, the change management part cannot be done by this role. For more information, see Change myth #4 in chapter 4.

If we want to be a purist, the Change Manager is not part of the Scrum Team. However, his or her position inside or outside does not really matter. An effective Product Owner will need a Change Manager to help him or her during all the phases of the project. The role of the Change Manager will be the same as in a waterfall model: drive change inside the organization and support the organization to drive change with the customer. In order to do so, the Change Manager will interact with the Scrum team to really understand the progress on the product development and how it may affect the change activities.

Now that we defined the place of the Change Manager in the Scrum team, let's turn our attention detailing each phase of the model.

CHAPTER 8: STEP-BY-STEP OVERVIEW – ROADMAP VISION

OBJECTIVES

From a project standpoint, we just have an idea or a problem statement to solve. If we look at our change model, this is just the beginning of the journey. The purpose of that phase will be to transform an unclear idea into requirements (called "user stories" or features in the Scrum lingo). Once again, the difference between the Waterfall and Agile models will be about the size of the requirements. In the waterfall methodology, the requirement will be completed at the end of the phase and will be difficult to change afterward.

In Scrum, the product end goals are defined in the product roadmap and the first set of requirements will be detailed in the product backlog. However, new requirements will be added as the project moves forward and some may be removed based on customers' feedbacks. During that phase, there are several outcomes that need to happen. We illustrate them in the following figure (as the one in the blue box):

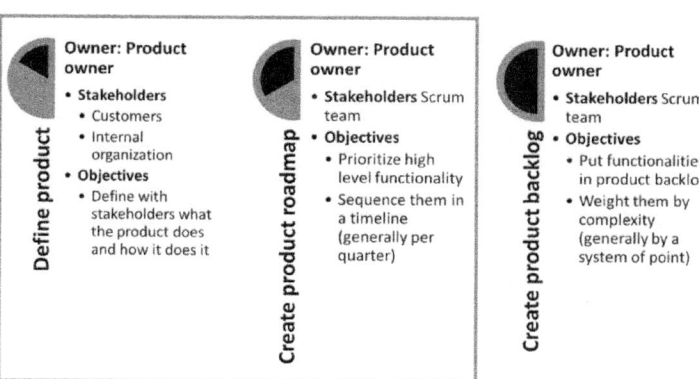

The purpose of the highlighted part is to clarify and organize the overall product idea into a workable data that will become the basis of the Product backlog later on. In addition, the product roadmap can be used to communicate to senior stakeholders inside the organization.

SCRUM TEAM

During this phase, there is no formal Scrum Team yet. We only have a Product Owner and a Change Manager. Their interaction is illustrated in the following figure:

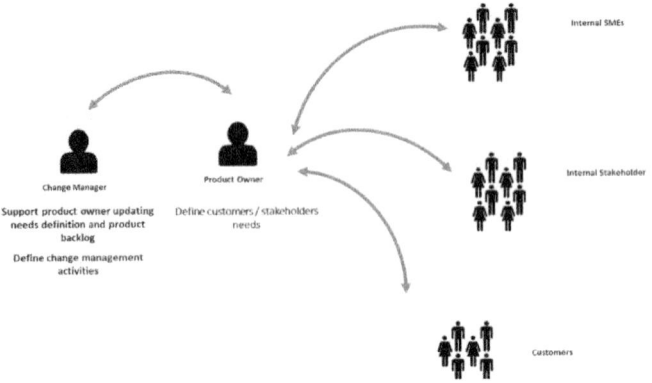

Internal SMEs

Internal Stakeholder

Customers

Change Manager

Support product owner updating
needs definition and product
backlog

Define change management
activities

Product Owner

Define customers / stakeholders
needs

ROLE OF THE CHANGE MANAGER

The role of the Change Manager during that phase can be divided into 2 categories: change activities and Product Owner support.

The first role is on the change side. The Change Manager needs to be associated with the clarification of the product idea into high-level user stories that will become the Product Roadmap and the Product Backlog. Even if he is not formally owning that phase, he needs to be informed as it will help him for his or her own tasks. He will be able to evaluate the change scope necessary to successfully deliver the product and as result, he can allocate his or her team resources accordingly. In addition, he can find the best tools and communication channels to support the project. We can illustrate that with the first gear of our new change model:

ROADMAP
VISION AND PLANNING FOR
CHANGE

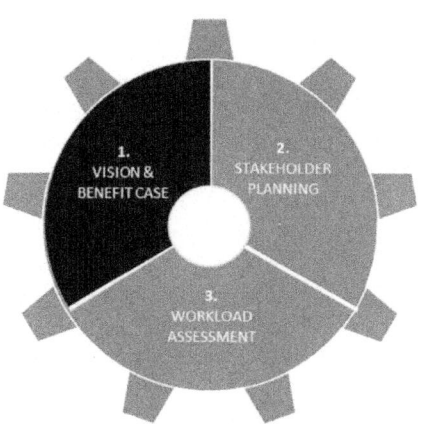

The Change Manager also has the informal role to support the Product Owner. An experienced Change

Manager in a company has his own network and as such can help a Product Owner to navigate in the organization. In addition, a Change Manager with several projects under his or her belt will normally be a trained facilitator. This skill can be useful for the Product Owner during meetings with stakeholders to ensure that they share all the necessary information to create valuable user stories.

MEETINGS FOR THE CHANGE MANAGER

There are no standard Scrum meetings during that phase. Therefore, the Product Owner needs to find the most effective way to gather the relevant and necessary information to properly define the product and provide the business case. The Change Manager should support him in that endeavor by participating in any meetings or events organized by the Product Owner. That would first include the product roadmap definition that will illustrate what the product does and when features will be developed. In addition, one role for the Product

Owner is to assign value (generally ROI if possible) for each user stories in order to prioritize them. The Change Manager needs to understand this part as it may affect the change strategy that he needs to develop.

CHANGE MODEL ARTIFACTS

In term of artifacts, the Change Manager will create the vision for change (with an elevator speech if necessary, a high-level impact assessment and the preliminary business case. Those 3 documents are the foundation of any project and product development. They also are the basis of any change management activity.

• **Change vision:** The change vision is the description of what your project is trying to achieve. It should reflect the pain points you are trying to solve and paint a vision of the "to-be situation" to ensure that the project is aligned with the company strategy.

• **High-level business impact:** This high-level business impact does not go into the detail as we are too early in the process. However, this is where the Change Manager starts to assess the impact on the organization (number of people affected, IT system to change....). with the help of the business. It will be one of the inputs for the benefits case.

• **Benefit case:** The benefits case is describing the tangible benefits of the project in term of Financial ROI, number of people impacted, new revenue generated. It will be the basis for the value realization plan that will measure the achievement of those objectives.

Those deliverables are necessary to convince senior stakeholders to move forward with the project. The input for their creation will be tightly linked to the product roadmap and the user stories evaluation. The Change Manager will work on the benefits case and value of the product on the behalf of the product owner. The product roadmap and the user story evaluation will be the primary input for the creation of an in-depth benefit case. He will also create the vision for change that can include an elevator speech to support early communication. The other artifact produced by the Change Manager is the business impact overview where the overall changes to the organization are described. This overview will later be detailed before each delivery to ensure that all aspects have been covered. This stage is critical even for products that are fully focused on customer use.

For example, a company wants to implement a new online platform for customers replacing basic mail and phone interaction with their customer service This product is directed towards the customer, but it would have a large internal impact. It may mean reorganization or even worse layoff in some parts of the business. Some of the internal monitoring execution processes may be completely different. Once live, only the more complex phone calls that cannot be solved by the online platform would be received by the customer service organization. Therefore, it may require the retraining and coaching of the remaining staff. As we see, this phase is critical and is the foundation of proper change management for the entire product lifecycle.

SUMMARY

We can summarize that phase in the following table:

Change manager Role	Meeting	Scrum outcome	Change Artifact
Informed	User story gathering	Product definition	Vision for change
Responsible	Vision creation	Product roadmap	Elevator speech
	User stories valuation	User story ROI	Initial business case
			Business impact assessment

CHAPTER 9: STEP-BY-STEP OVERVIEW – ROADMAP PLAN

OBJECTIVES

The purpose of this phase from a product development standpoint is to organize the development work and get started on creating the product with the first sprint. This is where the change strategy is developed and aligned with the Product Backlog. During the Product Backlog definition, the Development Team will estimate each user story. The outcome will be a Product Backlog where all stories are valued in benefits, estimated in development effort and sorted by priority.

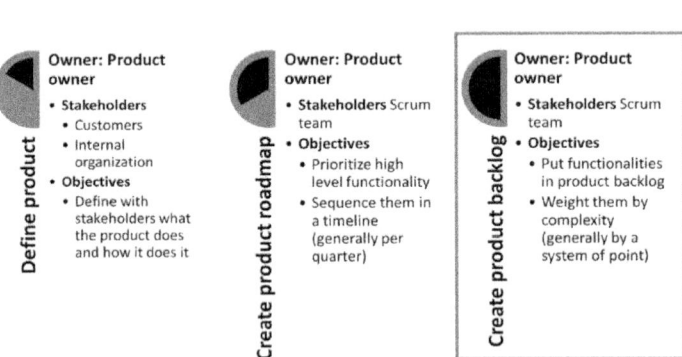

Define product

Owner: Product owner

- **Stakeholders**
  - Customers
  - Internal organization
- **Objectives**
  - Define with stakeholders what the product does and how it does it

Create product roadmap

Owner: Product owner

- **Stakeholders** Scrum team
- **Objectives**
  - Prioritize high level functionality
  - Sequence them in a timeline (generally per quarter)

Create product backlog

Owner: Product owner

- **Stakeholders** Scrum team
- **Objectives**
  - Put functionalities in product backlog
  - Weight them by complexity (generally by a system of point)

From a change management standpoint, the purpose of this phase is to understand the potential change management issues from both an organizational (organization not ready, unsuccessful past changes…) and leadership standpoint (who can drive or hinder the change). This information is a key element of the change management journey. It will drive all subsequent change actions for the project.

SCRUM TEAM

In the initiation phase, a Development Team is created and the Scrum Team (Product Owner, Scrum Master, and Development Team) is now complete as described below:

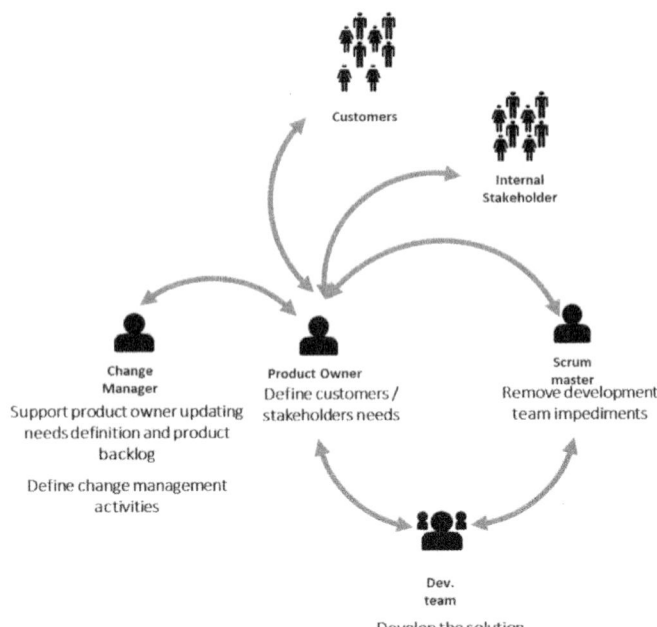

Customers

Internal
Stakeholder

Change
Manager
Support product owner updating
needs definition and product
backlog

Define change management
activities

Product Owner
Define customers /
stakeholders needs

Scrum
master
Remove development
team impediments

Dev.
team
Develop the solution

From that point onward, the team structure stays identical.

ROLE OF THE CHANGE MANAGER

The role of the Change Manager is to translate the product Backlog into a change management strategy. It's very close to the role he or she has in a waterfall model. This is the second part of our Agile Change Model:

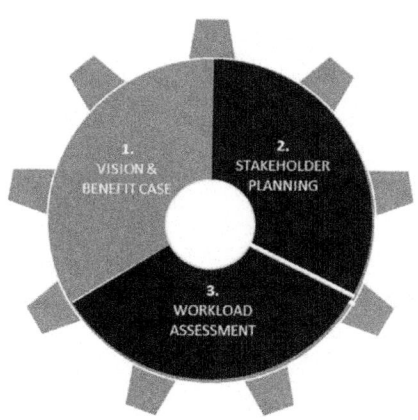

ROADMAP
VISION AND PLANNING FOR CHANGE

MEETINGS FOR THE CHANGE MANAGER

To execute that "translation", the most important meeting for the Change Manager will be the Product Backlog grooming meeting. Even if he is not a mandatory participant, during that meeting, the Change Manager will understand the overall priorities of user stories. In addition, he should also attend every sprint planning meeting as an observer to fully understand the functionalities that will be developed during the sprint. It will help him to adapt the content of the change strategy to the real execution of each sprint.

CHANGE MODEL ARTIFACTS

During this phase, the Change Manager will focus his or her attention on to a full understanding of the stakeholder landscape. He will organize several sessions with the project team and selected stakeholders to define three artifacts:

• **Complete stakeholder map:** A stakeholder map lists all the impacted stakeholders of a project and assesses their potential resistance to the project as well as their importance or influence inside the organization. It is generally a confidential document as some of its content could be perceived as shedding some unflattering light on some senior executives. It leads then to a change plan which will cater to those resistances.

• **In-depth change plan:** This document would describe what you should do and when you should do it to embed change inside the organization. It will include both your communication and your training plan.

• **Training plan:** This is the first plan to organize the training activities from training design, channel, resources allocation, and timing. It can be part of the change plan. This plan can be refined based on the feedback from an internal training organization.

Summary

The summary table looks like this:

Role	Meeting	Scrum outcome	Artifact
Informed	Product backlog meeting	Product Backlog	Change strategy
Informed	Sprint planning	Sprint backlog	Change load for the receiving organization

CHAPTER 10: STEP-BY-STEP OVERVIEW – DEVELOPMENT

The development will take place during sprints illustrated in the following manner (More references are given in chap. 5):

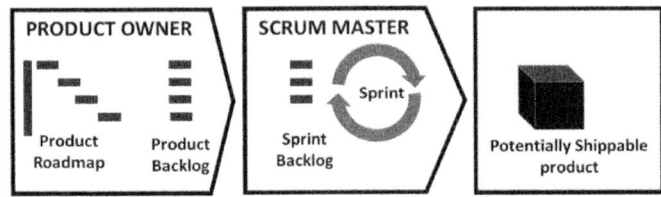

From a change standpoint, we can add a new gear to our change model:

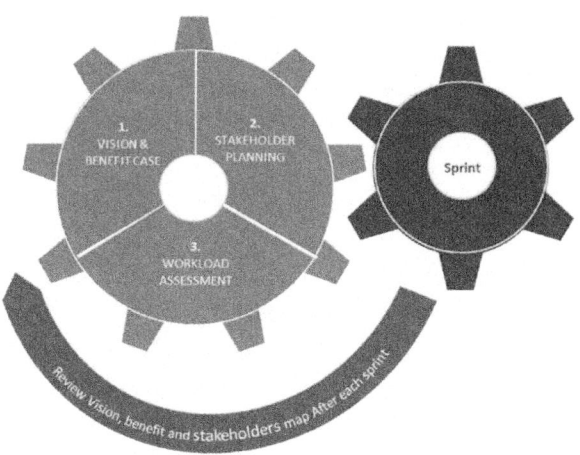

ROADMAP
VISION AND PLANNING FOR
CHANGE

DEVELOPPMENT
DEVELOP CHANGE

The small cycle arrow placed underneath the Roadmap wheel means that the iterative sprint process will have an impact on some of the artifacts developed like the Stakeholder map and the Business Case and even (but more rarely) the Change Vision in case of drastic change.

ROLE OF THE CHANGE MANAGER

The Change Manager will support the product development by working with the Product Owner on customers' and stakeholders' feedbacks during or at the end of the sprint. He also should be close to the Development Team and the Scrum Master during the sprint to understand the status of the development (thought the burn down chart for example).

The sprint review meeting is of the utmost importance for the Change Manager to attend. Indeed, during that meeting, a demo of the increment (or Minimum viable product) will be done. It will be the moment for representatives of the business and the customers to attend the demo and prepare the release phase. The Scrum guidelines require that key stakeholders attend the meeting to give proper feedback. It includes representatives (through a reference group for example as stated earlier) of the users, any legal or compliance officers and probably representatives of the customers.

Meetings for the Change Manager

During the sprint, the Change Manager can organize an intermediary and quick review meeting in relationship with the Scrum Master and Product Owner. The objective will be to ensure the preparation of proper information sharing with key stakeholders. The end goal will be the absence of surprise from those stakeholders during the Sprint review meeting.

Change Model artifacts

There will be a positive impact on the artifacts produced by the Change Manager as the notion of gap assessment will take place after each sprint. As such, the previously large gap assessment waterfall events and documents can be eliminated.

First, at the end of the sprint review, the Product Backlog is revised. It means that the improvements, the correction, the customer or stakeholder feedbacks will create new user stories or features to be prioritized and included in the product backlog. Non-developed or revised priorities will also affect the product backlog. For the next sprint, they may be integrated into the sprint planning meeting. As such there will be no artifacts about impact assessment as the feedback will directly be integrated. Based on the results of the sprint review, the Change Manager may revise his change strategy to adapt it to the revision of the Product Backlog. Indeed, if some features are pushed later in the roadmap, then the focus on certain stakeholders may change accordingly. In addition, the Change manager will review and possibly amend the change vision (rarely) in case of drastic changes and the Business benefits (more likely) as new features may bring new benefits.

Summary

We can sum that phase up in the summary phase:

Role	Meeting	Agile outcome	Artifact
Informed	Sprint review	Reviewed Product Backlog	Minimum Viable Change Plan
		New Sprint Backlog	Review of Stakeholder map (and Change Strategy), Benefit Case and Change vision
		Updated release backlog	

CHAPTER 11: STEP-BY-STEP OVERVIEW – DELIVERY

This phase is the bulk of the Change Manager works. It moves the product from the development world to the business organization or the customer. As we are assuming that we will release our product in increments, we can illustrate a backlog delivery like the graph below:

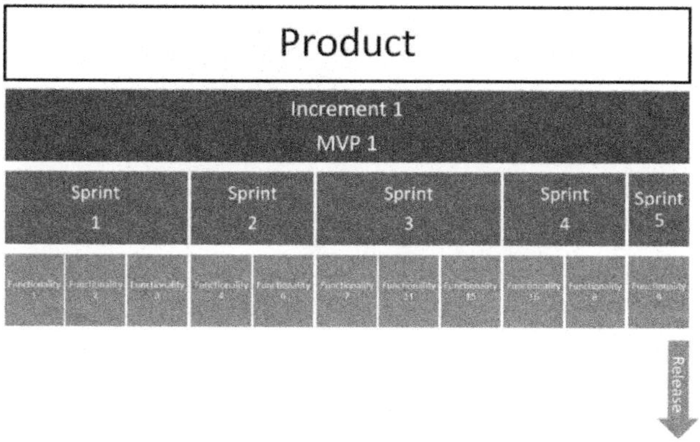

It has 3 main components that can be executed in parallel: organizational engagement, training and UAT (User Acceptance Testing) and Go Live. We need to add the final wheel to our model:

DELIVERY
ACTIVATE CHANGE

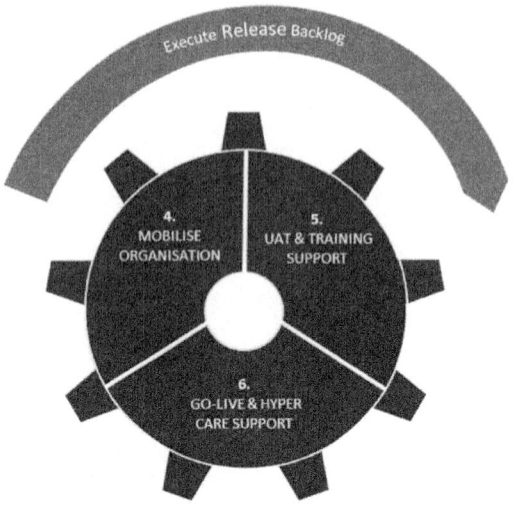

The Agile change model is now complete:

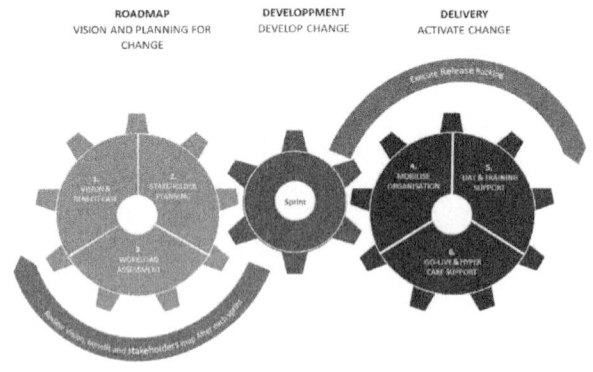

SCRUM TEAM

During the delivery, only the Product Owner is involved as the Scrum Manager and Development Team are focusing on the current sprint development as summarized below:

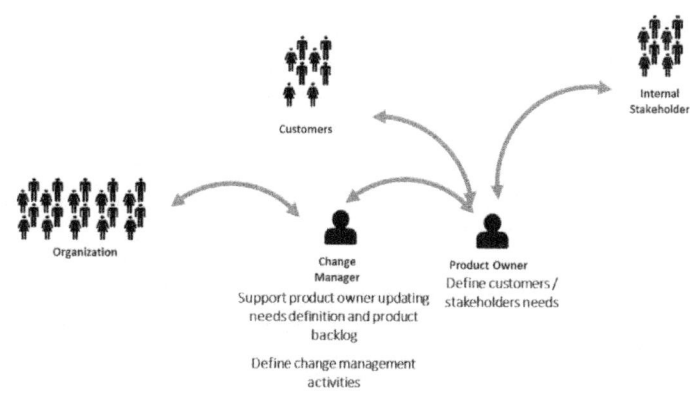

ROLE OF THE CHANGE MANAGER

During the delivery phase, the Change Manager interacts mainly with the Product Owner and the receiving organization. In the case of backlog release, the Change Manager role will not change compared to a waterfall approach. He or she will take care of the mobilization of the organization, work with the organization on UAT in case there is a need for it. We need to remember that each sprint has delivered a shippable product (a product that can be fully used by an internal user or the customer). Therefore, the need for User Acceptance Test should be minimal. Nevertheless, for highly critical application, a final User Acceptance Test would be preferable or required.

MEETINGS FOR THE CHANGE MANAGER

As the delivery is outside the standard Scrum model, there is no standard meeting for the Change Manager to attend.

CHANGE MODEL ARTIFACTS

ORGANIZATIONAL ENGAGEMENT

When the development is ready and signed off, you engage the organization. This is when your readiness activities come into play. However, comparing with a Waterfall approach, the Change Manager will only focus on the subset of the stakeholders that are affected by the release increment... We could call that a Minimum Viable Change Plan mirroring the notion of Minimum Viable Product.

During that phase, you will focus on internal communication, secure local resources to help the change.... In addition, you will measure how the perception of the project is evolving as those activities are conducted. This will help to ensure that the change management is on the right track.

This is also during that phase that the rollout strategy can be designed or refined. For major roll out in several countries (for example), a big bang option may not be the best option. During that exercise, the Change Managers will work with key stakeholders (internally and externally) to define the best approach. In the one of the major roll-out I was involved in, we released a very large software application in 160 countries region after region. It allowed to ensure the system stability in real-time and ensure that early bugs were corrected. After the first one, each region would start the system every 2 weeks, one after the other. It allowed us to postpone the last 3 regions as we realized that some backend software was not able to absorb the workload. Once the corrections were made, we could move forward with our roll-out.

• **Readiness plan:** The readiness plan encompasses all readiness activities that need to be performed by the organization to increase the chance of success. It also details how you measure it. Readiness can be measured by a survey (see next point) and/or task tracking. The benefit of having data is that you can give input to senior stakeholders on the organizational readiness and provide accurate input to Go/No Go meetings to prevent an early and costly roll out.

• **Readiness survey:** This is a classical tool to measure change readiness. You create a short online survey (to ensure participation). The questions are around the perception of the project (do you think the project will be a success?) and the individual feeling about the coming change (Am I confident that I can execute my new task after the Go Live?). In preparation for the start of the new product or software, this survey is conducted multiples times. If everything is going according to the change plan, the results should progress with a good perception of the project and a strong individual change commitment.

USER ACCEPTANCE TESTING AND TRAINING

This phase is critical as it is the last testing before the roll-out. In addition, it will be the period where the organization will be trained to use the product. There is no specific artifact during that phase. The only document is a training tracking mechanism to ensure that the training is disseminated at the proper pace inside the receiving organization. It will be part of the readiness plan.

GO LIVE

Go Live is the time when users or customers start to use your product. In the real live example described here, we have a period that is called Hypercare or Early Life Support. During that phase, a release team is tightly monitoring usage, performance, and issues of the new product.

• **Post start-up assessment:** After start-up, during the next few weeks or months, you will spend time ironing out the kinks and bring user feedbacks to the team. In that case, you will need to track that information in a document, which can also be used to update the organization about the issue resolution.

• **Benefit realization:** Based on the benefits case defined earlier, you track benefit realization. It should contain what you will measure but more importantly how you will do it. This is where you need to define if you have all the necessary reports or if you need additional data to be created. It will also describe who will run those measurements and how often they will be run. Once you get started you will measure the actual benefits of the project based on the value realization plan that you designed and refined during the project lifecycle.

After the new product is launched, you will have the early high-frequency monitoring, issue logs from internal users or customers. In the example mentioned above, we had twice-daily calls with selected users to feedback all issues and communication on the current resolution. Those actions and artifacts will still be used in the same manner as in the waterfall- managed project.

SUMMARY

The summary table will be as follows:

Role	Meeting	Scrum outcome	Artifact
Responsible	No standard Scrum meeting	No specific Scrum outcome	Training plan Readiness plan Readiness survey Readiness communication Go-to-Market strategy Issue log post Go Live

CHAPTER 12: SUMMARY

As we can see, even if some of the artifacts produced by the Change Manager do not drastically change, the speed of feedback and the number of reviews is greatly increased. On the flipside, some the artifacts that may have been perceived as bureaucratic and heavy are replaced by 2 or 3 backlogs (Product, Sprint and maybe Delivery) with associated decision-taking meetings. As such, a lot of the recording in change management documents become unnecessary in that setup. We can sum the entire change to the model in the below table:

Phase	Meeting	Scrum outcome	Change Artifact
Roadmap part 1	User story gathering meetings	Product definition	Vision for change
	Vision creation	Product roadmap	Elevator speech
	User stories valuation	User story ROI	Initial business case
			Business impact assessment

Roadmap part 2	Product backlog meeting	Product Backlog	Change strategy Change load for the receiving organization
Dev.	Sprint review	Reviewed Product Backlog	Minimum Viable Change Plan Review of Stakeholder map (and Change Strategy), Benefit Case and Change vision
Delivery	No standard Scrum meeting	No specific Scrum outcome	Training plan Readiness plan Readiness survey Readiness communication

			Go-to-Market strategy
			Issue log post Go Live

The second impact is that new change model is not linear and focus on iteration of steps 1,2.3 (per sprint) and 4,5,6 (per release). It is worthwhile to also note that those iterations can also happen in parallel as the sprints do not stop during a release. It means that the Change Manager will have to review and amend his vision for change (rarely), stakeholder map and business case (more frequently) while supporting the delivery focusing on business impact, mobilizing the organization, set up training, and UAT and going live. As such we need to have a new visualization for that model:

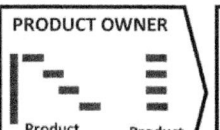
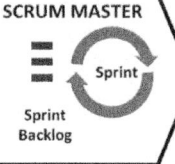

PRODUCT OWNER

Product Roadmap — Product Backlog

SCRUM MASTER

Sprint Backlog — Sprint

PRODUCT OWNER

Potentially Shippable product

ROADMAP
VISION AND PLANNING FOR CHANGE

DEVELOPPMENT
DEVELOP CHANGE

DELIVERY
ACTIVATE CHANGE

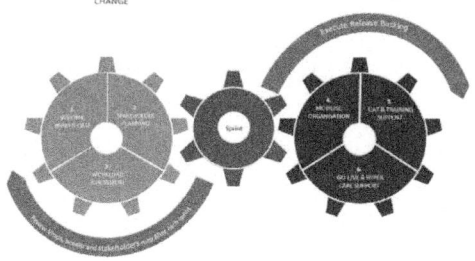

CHAPTER 13: MULTI-TEAM PRODUCT DEVELOPMENT

We all know that the vast majority of projects cannot be done by a single team of 7 to 9 people in one location. They involve several teams that are sometimes not even collocated. The purpose of the following chapter is to see how the Change Manager will interact with the team(s) in that environment. We will review that concerns through the lens of the 2 main organizational frameworks: LeSS and SAFe.

SCALED MODELS

From an Agile framework point of view, both SAFe and LeSS are very similar. The main difference will be in the overall environment. LeSS will be leaner and more flexible but will require more maturity to be executed. SAFe will be more "administrative" by adding some PMO function and the notion of Release Train coupling different teams. We will not delve into a precise description of those frameworks as this not the core of this books.

From a large product standpoint, both systems arrive at the same conclusion: large projects are too big for a single Product Owner. To solve that conundrum while keeping unity and integrity of the product development, a team of Product Owner will be created reporting to a "top" Product Owner. Those Product Owners will be with their own Scrum Team(s) and their Product Backlog will be a subset of the master one.

For LeSS, the Product Owner spends time working with the Scrum Teams, in the same manner, he or she would do with a single one. However, he or she will use a "relay" inside each Scrum Team called Area Product Owner. The "top" Product Owner is a coordinator not only between the teams but also with the customers and various stakeholders. He or she also owns one Product Backlog supporting the whole product. However, this backlog will be split among all the Area Product Owner to ensure proper ownership. This function is even more demanding than a classical Product Owner and as such cannot be given to an inexperienced Product Owner.

SAFe is introducing the concept of the Product Manager that is somewhat of a hybrid between a Classical Product Owner and a Program Manager. He or she will manage a team of Product Owners. The Product Manager will focus on the work before the sprint and during the release. Before the sprint, he or she will be in charge of the Vision and the Product Roadmap. In the end, he or she will be more focused on the release to the final customer. In that specific setup, the Change Manager will work directly with him or her on those phases.

THE ROLE OF THE CHANGE MANAGER

In both cases, we have a "top" Product Owner in charge, whatever the names that he or she is given. This role focuses more on activities that happen before the first sprint (product definition) and during the release as the detail of the development will be managed at the product Owner team level (as seen in both graphs below). He or she will be more in charge of the Vision, and the Product Roadmap and focus more on the release to the final customer. That does not mean that everything stops during the sprints. During the development phase, the top Product Owner will obviously still work with the stakeholders to refine and amend the Product Backlog and ensure that the teams are properly coordinated. Finally, as a team leader, he or she will have a coaching function to guide his or her team.

In that specific setup, the Change Manager will work directly with him or her on those phases. Indeed, if we remember the revised change model graph, most of the work of the Change manager happens during those phases. Those are the activities 1,2,3 before the first sprints and 4,5,6,7 before and during the release. In a sense, this is in line with the revised change model proposed in the previous chapter but at the next level.

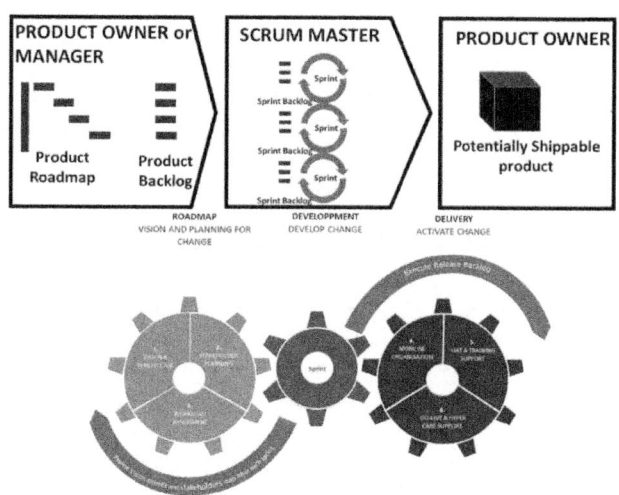

CONCLUSION

As we can see, a large-scale model neither changes the role of the Change manager in Agile nor impacts revised change model that we defined at the end of the previous chapter. However, to support a large-scale project impacting various internal or external stakeholders in different functions and geographies, a change team supporting the Change Manager may be necessary. In that case, the structure of the Business Change would mirror the one from the Product Owner team.

CHAPTER 15: HOW TO CHANGE YOUR CURRENT MODEL

A 7-STEP PROCESS

If your company is transforming itself using Scrum or another Agile framework, it means that you were working with waterfall before. In that case, the change managers most likely used an existing change framework linked to that model. It would neither be realistic not value-added to start from scratch a new change model, so you will have to adapt your existing one: This paragraph proposes a blueprint on how to execute that transformation. This 7-step process is illustrated below:

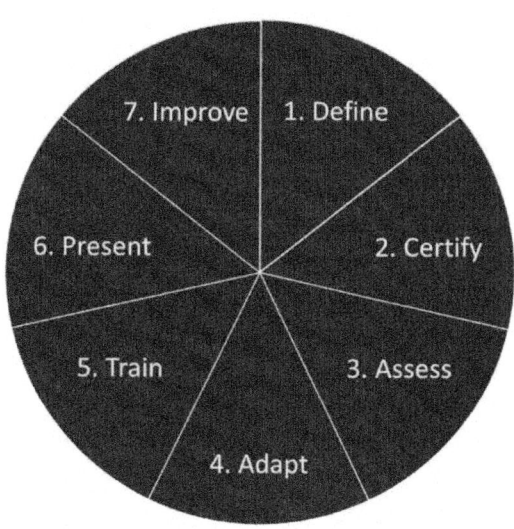

DEFINE

If the project development model changes, the new Agile framework needs to be presented to the change team as they need to understand which Agile framework has been chosen, the process steps, the roles and responsibility, and the expectation for the Change Management team.

In any company, defining the Agile model used and implementing its execution is the charge a specific team or specific managers. The Change team should organize a workshop with them to have this new approach presented. This would also be the time for questions and clarification with the relevant experts.

CERTIFY

In any team, you have people who are more thinker and people that are more action-based. You will need to train and certify your more experienced thinkers as they will spearhead the change model transformation effort. Based on my experience, it is valuable to certify them both as Product Owner and Scrum Master. Indeed, as scrum does not talk about change, fully understanding those functions gives a perfect view on what will be expected from the Change Manager. This approach would work for every Agile framework used.

ASSESS

Once the certification is completed, this advanced group will assess the impacts on the change model. Those impacts can be threefold: neutral (no impact), negative (more complex work, more frequent delivery, new tools, and meetings...) or positive (simpler documents, suppression of certain deliverables....). It will be a relatively long and tedious task to define what to keep and remove but most importantly, which artifacts need to be modified. The point of this phase is also to modify them to have them ready to be used. At the end of that phase, the team should have the first "shippable product" for its new change model.

ADAPT

Once the assessment is done, then the actions to adapt the model will be clear. The challenge will be to execute them as fast as possible while performing day-to-day duties. During that phase, I would advocate an Agile mindset and frequent interactions with your internal customers (the ones that will use your services) to ensure the alignment between the model developed and the internal customers' needs. Once again the experts mentioned in part 1 are the necessary sparring partners to ensure that your model first the bill.

TRAIN

As the new model is fully developed, you need to train your entire team to ensure a consistent service delivery. You could also develop a system of mentoring where the advanced team can support the rest of the team and play the role of expert.

PRESENT

This is the time where you present your new model to the product organization. This is a final presentation but the several previous interactions during the "Adapt" phase should prevent any misalignment and avoid any surprise.

IMPROVE

Any model (especially a new one) can and should be improved. That is the Agile spirit. You should set aside time with your team after 1 to 2 releases to define the areas of improvements and put in place the necessary action to close the gap.

CONCLUSION

Transforming an existing model is not difficult, but it is necessary for 2 reasons. The first one is a matter of efficiency. Indeed, to deliver on future product, the change team needs to stay relevant and provide a service adapted to the development process. The second reason is more about perception. As change management is not defined in the Agile model, there will be a temptation to see the change team as irrelevant in the new landscape. By being proactive and adapt your model beforehand, you can mitigate that risk and ensure that future product development will have proper change management attached to them.

CHAPTER 16: ONE YEAR LATER

We are now more than a year in our Agile journey, this may be time to add some learnings. We will focus in this chapter on 3 items that affected (and are still prevalent) us as we were progressing toward a more agile setup: Agile transition, Change fatigue, and the introduction of the customer.

AGILE TRANSITION

The transformation of any company towards an Agile setup is not something that can be done overnight. Several things need to be settled to achieve the new state. First, you need to choose your model. Will you go for Scrum or if you are a large company; SAFe or LeSS? Before this choice (and sometimes even after) is officially made you may have several "chapels" competing. The only silver lining is that a Scrum (or a variant of it) will happen in the process. Then people need to be trained and internal processes need to be changed (budget, program review….).

How do you manage during this period? The only option is to be pragmatic and not expect a perfect setup from day one. However, the challenge will be to balance that pragmatism with some non-negotiable items that, if not applied, would alter the final objective. The best way is to ask for help (internally or externally) from Agile experts that can advise as you progress toward your agile goal.

But regardless of the support that you may have, this will be a challenging time for your team as they also try to gain experience dealing with Agile. As such, keeping frequent meetings and being very sensitive to the team mood and engagement will be critical mitigating the stress.

CHANGE FATIGUE

As we saw in the previous chapter, Agile does not change that much the change process but decreases the batch size and increases the frequency. It means that your receiving organization will face an onslaught of change coming their way. Even in case of backlog release (let's say every quarter), in between the release themselves and the bug corrections, there will be new things every week or so. Besides, large companies generally have several products being created at the same time. It may mean that several times per week, minor or major changes will be generated in the product landscape.

How do you manage that? First, let's be realistic, you can only mitigate that factor. If you are even a moderate phone app user, you know that updates are coming your way several times a week. This is the new normal. However, that does not mean that you cannot mitigate the situation. The first thing to do is for each product to split the major release and the minor bug corrections. If the bug corrections are not critical, group them and release them on a set schedule or even wait (if you can) for the next release. The second thing is to use your change leaders and create a coordination mechanism among them so that they can discuss when is the best time to communicate with their stakeholders.

A NEW DIFFERENT STAKEHOLDER: THE CUSTOMER

With the advent of digital, major parts of B2B processes are on their way to "be outsourced to the customer". The B2C industries went that way one or two decades ago and the B2B world is now following. Several consulting companies (Gartner, McKinsey) are predicting that by 2030, even major "asset focused" B2B companies (like mining) will transition part of their process in the digital world with external customers. This is a completely different world than the one we lived in a few decades ago where the major stakeholders were internal. Managing them was finally simple from a logistical standpoint as they work in the same company. You have some control over their schedule, better ability to gather data or to create events...With customers, it is a different game and your ability to gather needs or drive tool adoption is more limited. In addition, the work required is different if you are trying to gather user stories or driving adoption.

If you are trying to define a new product or gather new requirements on an existing one, you can work with external companies that focus on integrating customer involvement at each step of the development cycle. First, they generally have databases of customers that they can reach out or they can use your customers' base to target relevant customers. Once done, they are specialized in gathering and analyzing the information given. Certain large companies have also insourced that skillset by creating "Insight" teams doing the same thing.

If you are working on driving adoption, you need to create a set of skills inside the teams that are working with your customer (generally Customer Service teams), so that those teams can actively "sell" the benefits of the new tools each time they have a contact with a customer. This is a change of focus that will require time for the organization to accept and align with and can only be driven by the company leadership. It needs to happen even though some of the tools may threaten existing jobs inside the organization. As the organization needs to accept this new reality, it means that some of their employees' time will be dedicated to those "selling' tasks. This change of work content and skills will require more change management on that new focus.

CHAPTER 17: ONE MORE THING

Since Steve Jobs, the "one more thing" tagline has become something that indicates new important things that are coming up. As stated earlier in the book, Agile is a new field and is changing fast. One thing related to Agile development became popular recently and will have an impact on the world of a Change Manager: Design thinking. Before we look at the impact on the change role in product development, let's examine what are these concepts and how they fit in the Agile development process.

WHAT IS DESIGN THINKING

A QUICK HISTORICAL PERSPECTIVE

In the 50s and 60s, new ideas about development morphed into design thinking as a problem-solving process. John E. Arnold can be considered as one of the pioneers in "Creative Engineering" (which introduced the concept of "Design Thinking"). Another one of the founding fathers is L. Bruce Archer in his book: "Systematic Method for Designers".

In the 50's, Arnold defined four uses for design thinking. It's a finding tool allowing to design a solution for a new need, a new solution to an existing need, a more effective solution for an existing problem or a solution that would lead to better sales (even if that last one could be also overlapping with point #2 and point #3).

L. Bruce Archer's "Systematic Method for Designers" was written in 1965 and focused on systematizing the designing process, he realized the need to expand on its original scope. In this book, he added the following characteristics for Design Thinking::

"Ways have had to be found to incorporate knowledge of ergonomics, cybernetics, marketing, and management science into design thinking".

Building on those 2 pioneers, the notion of design as "way of thinking" was expanded by Herbert A. Simon's 1969 book "The Sciences of the Artificial" and McKim's 1973 book "Experiences in Visual Thinking." In the 80s, architecture was at the forefront of design thinking with Bryan Lawson's "How Designers Think" and Nigel Cross' article on "Designerly ways of knowing". Those works defined the basic features of design thinking.

In the 90s, Rolf Faste built on the early McKim's work at Stanford by teaching design thinking as a way to act and create solutions. David M. Kelley (a colleague of Rolf Faste at Stanford), founded the renowned design consultancy IDEO in 1991 and transferred the notion of design thinking into the business world.

VARIOUS REPRESENTATION

There is no single representation of the design thinking process, even though we can find commonalities in some of the major frameworks.

THE DESIGN BRITISH COUNCIL DOUBLE DIAMOND

The British Design Council illustrates the Design Thinking process with the Double Diamond model in the following manner:

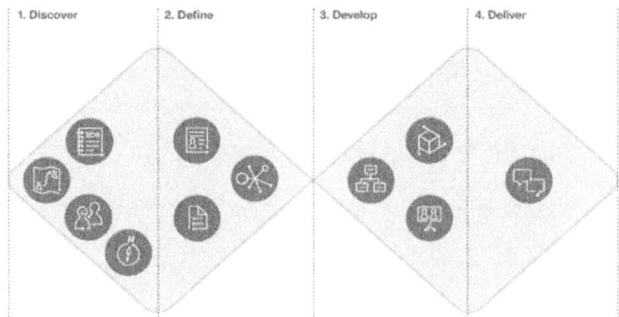

This model is split into four distinct phases – Discover, Define, Develop and Deliver. The Diamond illustrates the fact that all creative processes work in a divergent/convergent framework. As they state on their website:

"In all creative processes a number of possible ideas are created ('divergent thinking') before refining and narrowing down to the best idea ('convergent thinking'), and this can be represented by a diamond shape. But the Double Diamond indicates that this happens twice – once to confirm the problem definition and once to create the solution. One of the greatest mistakes is to omit the left-hand diamond and end up solving the wrong problem."

Different tools (user diaries, journey mapping, and character profiles…) support each phase to collect the maximum ideas possible (divergent phase) and then refining and narrowing the best ones (converging phase).

During the "Discover" phase, the group will try to understand reality through various lenses, trying to see the world not only as it is but also in a new way (with less bias or preconceived notions for example). The "Define" phase it trying to make sense of all the data that were gathered during the "Discover" phase and prioritize them. At the end of that phase, the problem that the team is trying to solve is properly framed to start the "Develop" phase. This phase is where concepts are created, refined and solution are found for the problem statement framed earlier. Finally, the "Delivery" is where the final product is launched.

This model was developed by the d.School at Stanford University (School of Design). It looks different but we find again the similar steps.

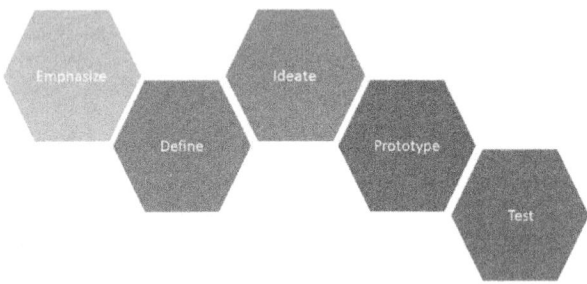

THE "DESIGN FOR GROWTH" MODEL

The information below is coming from an excellent book describing what Design thinking is. The content is even overlapping with the Lean startup part. In this book, written by Jeanne Liedtka and Tim Ogilvie, we discover a structured process to extract and start solving pain points for the customers with a new physical product, new process or a new software…

This is process is in 4 phases: "what is", "what if", "what wows" and "what works". In my opinion, the last phase is close to the "Lean Start-up" where we prototype, select one or several solutions before refining them. In the book, this process is modeled in the following way:

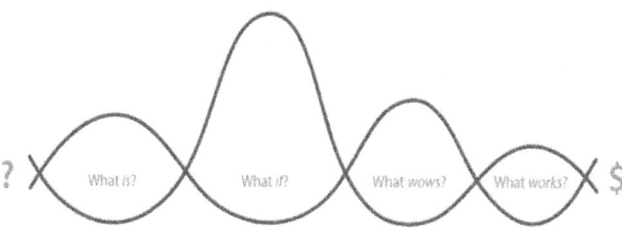

As we can see, all those phases seem to diverge before converging. This is by design as each phase to open understanding before we can assess and narrow it to useful information. Let's focus on the phases used during that process. It will be helpful later to assess the impact on our model and the role of the Change Manager.

What is: This is the data-gathering phase where reality is dissected the scrutinized to ensure a proper understanding of the real issues that are faced by the customers.

What if: During that phase, we are imagining what could be. This is a dreaded phase by business leaders as everyone remembers useless brainstorming sessions that went nowhere or just justified decisions that were already taken. However, brainstorming is just one of the tools (not THE tool) used during that phase, but, more importantly, a well-managed one is necessary to really propose innovative solutions to a well-framed issue.

What Wows: This is the final step (before the "what works") where you narrow your potential solutions to the one that will have the most impact on the issue you are trying to solve.

What works: This last phase is about prototyping and defining (defining) the final solution. However, in some models (like the Gartner one below), this phase is extracted from the Design Thinking phase to become independent.

The link between tools and phases looks like that:

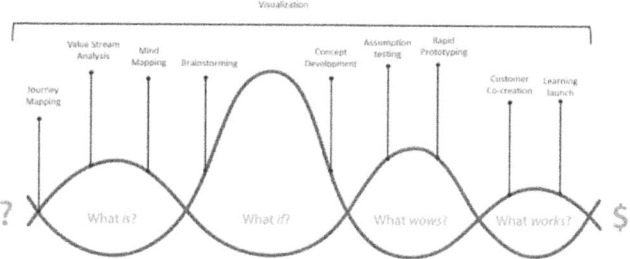

INTEGRATION WITH AGILE

Gartner tried to improve on those models by adding two important information that they felt were lacking. The first one is "how to prototype" and the second one is "where does Agile fit in?" As such, they attempted to develop the following holistic representation.

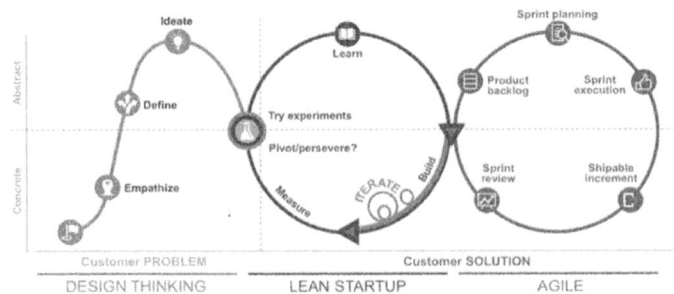

As we can see once the design and prototyping have been completed, then the Agile cycle kicks in to deliver a scaled solution to the customers.

ONE PROPOSED SINGLE MODEL

From that point onward, we will use some kind of "frankenmodel" put together with the best pieces from the models described above. This model has the benefit of the Gartner view which separates the 3 product development phases and put Agile in the picture. It has the double diamond mindset used during the early stage of the design thinking as those phases will work with a diverging/converging thinking approach. Finally, it uses the process defined in the "Design for Growth" model which clearly lay out the way to approach design thinking.

IMPACT ON CHANGE MANAGEMENT

AN IMPROVED CHANGE FRAMEWORK

If we remember our model with the 3 gears, the first step was dedicated to creating and sharing a vision. As we can see this step is now the sole focus of the design thinking phase. In that case, I would propose that we break down the first wheel in two parts and create a vision wheel to create a revised model:

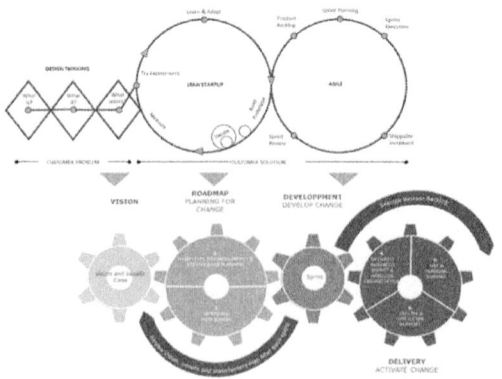

As we can see the model is not very different but its integration with the design thinking approach is more logical.

Impact on the Change Manager role

What does that mean? It means that the Change Manager needs to get involved in facilitating (or even in leading in some cases) the vision phase to capture and refine the vision for the product. If your company is using external or internal design studio, the Change lead can be one of the participants of the process as the necessary skillset would be readily available for that phase. In case there are no dedicated design resources available, then the Change Manager may lead that process. It means that he needs to be skilled enough to facilitate the session and trained enough to ensure a positive outcome. The alternative will be to bring in consultants, which may help to start the process but will increase the overall cost.

CONCLUSION

The field of change management is affected by the method of development used to create new products. It means that, as Change leaders, we need to constantly revise our skillset to stay relevant. We need also to adapt our models, not only based on those new activities, but also on the skills levels of the organization we are working for. As we saw, a Change manager may even have to lead some of the design thinking activities if the organization does not have the required skills available. This is an extremely exciting situation for our job but that will also come with its somewhat daunting challenges in term of adaptation.

FINAL WORDS

Agile is not a fad. It will impact project management and product development in the next decades. I can safely make that assumption because companies that will use it properly will have a competitive advantage and will be faster and more effective at rolling out products than their competitors. The same happened when Lean Manufacturing started to be perceived as the next frontier in the manufacturing process. Companies were surprised at first and Japanese cars started to take over the world. Some companies reacted successfully, and some did not. The ones that did not, were either closed or bought. This illustrates the basic way business works and was described in 1942 with the famous "creative destruction" coined by Joseph Schumpeter. So, if Agile is not a fad but is also very young, how does the change management field need to evolve to support an Agile product development or project? This question is at the heart of this book which tried to answer it.

The first 3 chapters of the book were about Agile management. We tried to bust myths and misunderstandings about Agile. We answered the question: what it is and what it's not? We described the current frameworks used and finally, we drilled down on the basics of almost all Agile models: The Scrum framework. The 2 next chapters focused on the role of change management and on some of the famous models used currently in the business landscape.

Once we established the context of both side of the coins, we could start to answer the question at the beginning of this book. As we could see, the change does not create a model drastically different in term of focus but really affects its execution. As we stated earlier in the book, we will not claim a definitive answer for two reasons. Firstly, every change model in every company (if your company is using one) is different. However, we hope that the thought process behind this book can help reproduce the same exercise. Secondly, Agile is a moving target, evolving constantly, mirroring in a sense the pace of evolution we are currently experiencing in the world. Therefore, the Agile frameworks will most likely be different in 2, 3 or 5 years. Therefore, the answer to the core question of the book will probably have evolved accordingly.

With the apparition of Agile frameworks, the roles of Change Managers may not be different, but the modus operandi will be transformed. As Change Managers, we should welcome change as it will bring amazing opportunities to rethink our role and our work. I can put that in the words of one of my former boss (and friend): "we need to drink our own Champaign". This is the only way to us to ensure we can still be relevant in our mission to support to company strategies around the world.

ADDENDUM

OFFICIAL SCRUM GLOSSARY

(from the Scrum.org website)

B

Burn-down Chart: A chart which shows the amount of work which is thought to remain in a backlog. Time is shown on the horizontal axis and work remaining on the vertical axis. As time progresses and items are drawn from the backlog and completed, a plot line showing work remaining may be expected to fall. The amount of work may be assessed in any of several ways such as user story points or task hours. Work remaining in Sprint Backlogs and Product Backlogs may be communicated by means of a burn-down chart. See also: Burnup Chart

Burn-up Chart: A chart which shows the amount of work which has been completed. Time is shown on the horizontal axis and work completed on the vertical axis. As time progresses and items are drawn from the backlog and completed, a plot line showing the work done may be expected to rise. The amount of work may be assessed in any of several ways such as user story points or task hours. The amount of work considered to be in-scope may also be plotted as a line; the burn-up can be expected to approach this line as work is completed.

C

Coherent/Coherence: The quality of the relationship between certain Product Backlog items which may make them worthy of consideration as a whole. See also: Sprint Goal.

D

Daily Scrum: Daily time-boxed event of 15 minutes, or less, for the Development Team to re-plan the next day of development work during a Sprint. Updates are reflected in the Sprint Backlog.

Definition of Done: A shared understanding of expectations that the Increment must live up to in order to be releasable into production. Managed by the Development Team.

Development Team: The role within a Scrum Team accountable for managing, organizing and doing all development work required to create a releasable Increment of product every Sprint.

E

Emergence: The process of the coming into existence or prominence of new facts or new knowledge of a fact, or knowledge of a fact becoming visible unexpectedly.

Empiricism: Process control type in which only the past is accepted as certain and in which decisions are based on observation, experience and experimentation. Empiricism has three pillars: transparency, inspection and adaptation.

Engineering standards: A shared set of development and technology standards that a Development Team applies to create releasable Increments of software.

F

Forecast (of functionality): The selection of items from the Product Backlog a Development Team deems feasible for implementation in a Sprint.

I

Increment: A piece of working software that adds to previously created Increments, where the sum of all Increments -as a whole- form a product.

P

Product Backlog: An ordered list of the work to be done in order to create, maintain and sustain a product. Managed by the Product Owner.

Product Backlog refinement: The activity in a Sprint through which the Product Owner and the Development Teams add granularity to the Product Backlog.

Product Owner: The role in Scrum accountable for maximizing the value of a product, primarily by incrementally managing and expressing business and functional expectations for a product to the Development Team(s).

R

Ready: A shared understanding by the Product Owner and the Development Team regarding the preferred level of description of Product Backlog items introduced at Sprint Planning.

Refinement: See Product Backlog Refinement

S

Scrum: A framework to support teams in complex product development. Scrum consists of Scrum Teams and their associated roles, events, artifacts, and rules, as defined in the Scrum Guide™.

Scrum Board: A physical board to visualize information for and by the Scrum Team, often used to manage Sprint Backlog. Scrum boards are an optional implementation within Scrum to make information visible.

Scrum Guide™: The definition of Scrum, written and provided by Ken Schwaber and Jeff Sutherland, co-creators of Scrum. This definition consists of Scrum's roles, events, artifacts, and the rules that bind them together.

Scrum Master: The role within a Scrum Team accountable for guiding, coaching, teaching and assisting a Scrum Team and its environments in a proper understanding and use of Scrum.

Scrum Team: A self-organizing team consisting of a Product Owner, Development Team and Scrum Master.

Scrum Values: A set of fundamental values and qualities underpinning the Scrum framework; commitment, focus, openness, respect and courage.

Self-organization: The management principle that teams autonomously organize their work. Self-organization happens within boundaries and against given goals. Teams choose how best to accomplish their work, rather than being directed by others outside the team.

Sprint: Time-boxed event of 30 days, or less, that serves as a container for the other Scrum events and activities. Sprints are done consecutively, without intermediate gaps.

Sprint Backlog: An overview of the development work to realize a Sprint's goal, typically a forecast of functionality and the work needed to deliver that functionality. Managed by the Development Team.

Sprint Goal: A short expression of the purpose of a Sprint, often a business problem that is addressed. Functionality might be adjusted during the Sprint in order to achieve the Sprint Goal.

Sprint Planning: Time-boxed event of 8 hours, or less, to start a Sprint. It serves for the Scrum Team to inspect the work from the Product Backlog that's most valuable to be done next and design that work into Sprint backlog.

Sprint Retrospective: Time-boxed event of 3 hours, or less, to end a Sprint. It serves for the Scrum Team to inspect the past Sprint and plan for improvements to be enacted during the next Sprint.

Sprint Review: Time-boxed event of 4 hours, or less, to conclude the development work of a Sprint. It serves for the Scrum Team and the stakeholders to inspect the Increment of product resulting from the Sprint, assess the impact of the work performed on overall progress and update the Product backlog in order to maximize the value of the next period.

Stakeholder: A person external to the Scrum Team with a specific interest in and knowledge of a product that is required for incremental discovery. Represented by the Product Owner and actively engaged with the Scrum Team at Sprint Review.

V

Values: When the values of Commitment, Courage, Focus, Openness and Respect are embodied and lived by the Scrum Team, the Scrum pillars of transparency, inspection, and adaptation come to life and builds trust for everyone. The Scrum Team members learn and explore those values as they work with the Scrum events, roles and artifacts.

Velocity: An optional, but often used, indication of the average amount of Product Backlog turned into an Increment of product during a Sprint by a Scrum Team, tracked by the Development Team for use within the Scrum Team.

CHANGE MANAGEMENT DOCUMENT EXAMPLES

This part is providing examples of documents that can be used by Change Managers. Their use is not mandatory, and they are only provided as illustration. Your company may have others format or additional documents.

ROADMAP VISION

Change vision preparatory document

The preparatory document is a list of questions that the Change Manager and the Product Owner need to ask themselves. The answers should always be targeted toward 3 constituents: the company, the customers, and the employees. Those questions will help build the final vision for change that should be presented to senior stakeholders.

1. **Audiences:** Who are the broad internal and external audiences we need to engage and excite about our product?

2. **Concerns:** What are their priorities and main concerns?

3. **Business pains?** Which audience and business pains do we address?

4. **Benefits audience:** Which audience and business benefits do we provide? (focus on 3 sub-categories: customers, company, employee)

5. **Changes:** What are we changing to reach the benefits?

6. **Recap:** Why should our audiences care?

7. **Link to strategy:** How does the product tie into the overall company strategy?

Change vision

This can be only a 2 slides documents based on the key messages you defined after the questions from the preparatory document.

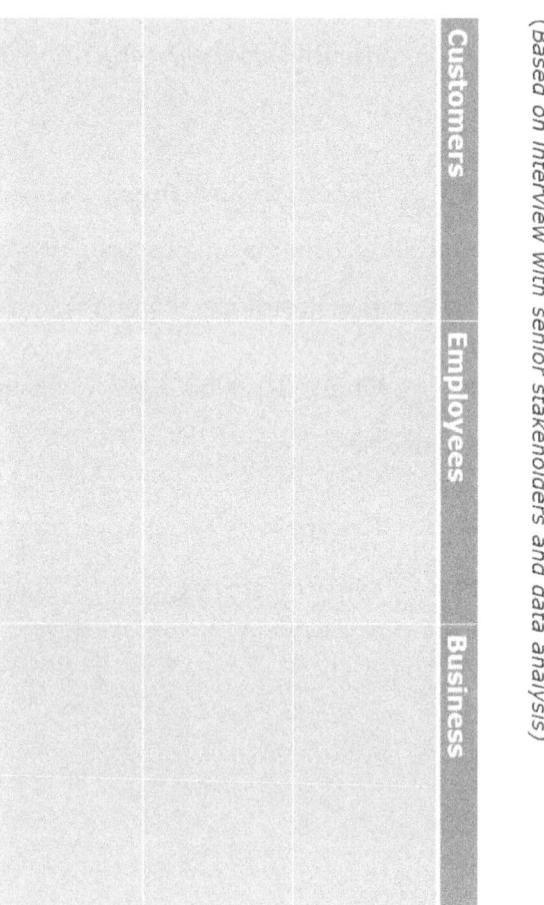

Product XXX

Customer benefits
Benefit 1
Benefit 2

Business benefits
Benefit 1
Benefit 2

Employee benefits
Benefit 1
Benefit 2

Expected outcome
Describe outcome

Vision for change
*Describe the vision for
change*

How to get there
*Describe the path to
reach the benefits
(organizational changes,
IT changes, process
changes....)*

High-level business impact

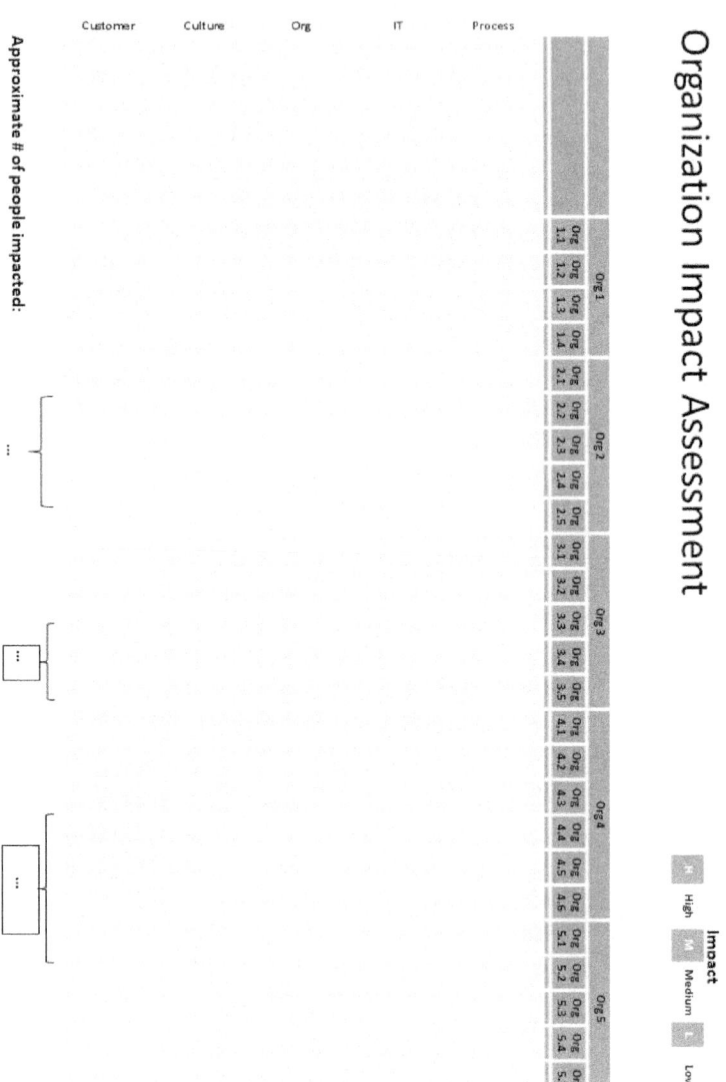

Benefit case

There are 5 topics that a proper business case should have in order for senior stakeholders to make an informed decision on the way forward:

1. **Program/Project description:** This topic recap the overall program/project/product objectives, expected benefits.

2. **Costs:** This part would cover the overall program/project/product cost including consultant, IT (software/hardware), internal resources, operating cost (travel, workshop....)

3. **Benefits:** This is where the measurable benefits need to be inputted. Based on those benefits, measurable KPIs and a tracker will be designed for post-Go Live measurement.

4. **Investment case:** Based on those 2 previous items, you can calculate the ROI or payback time of the project/program/product.

5. **Risks:** This is a view on all the possible risks from a business, IT, processes, employees, organization need to be recorded.

Complete stakeholder map

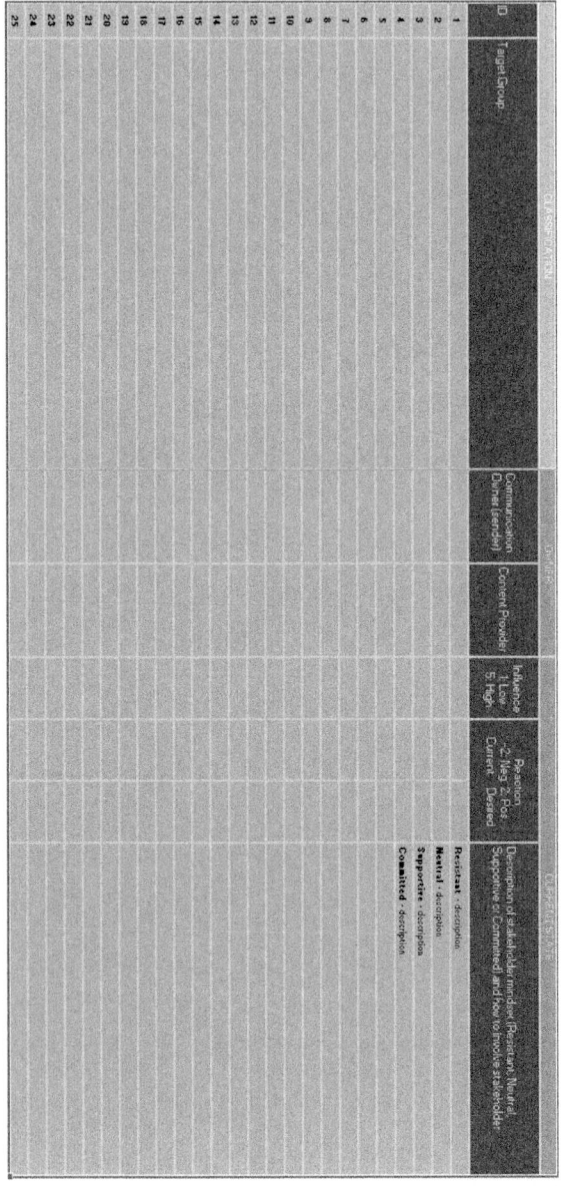

Stakeholder Map

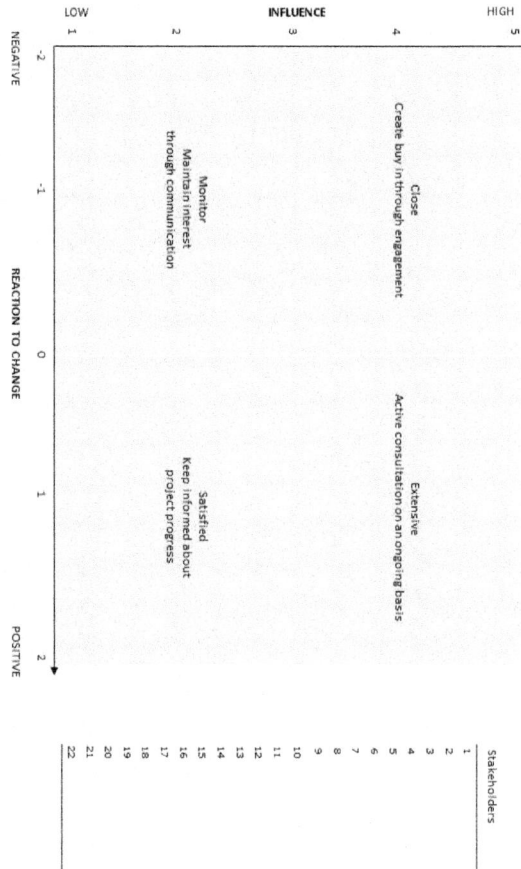

LOW	INFLUENCE			HIGH
1	2	3	4	5

NEGATIVE   -2   -1   0   1   2   POSITIVE

REACTION TO CHANGE

Close
Create buy in through engagement

Extensive
Active consultation on an ongoing basis

Monitor
Maintain interest
through communication

Satisfied
Keep informed about
project progress

Stakeholders

1
2
3
4
5
6
7
8
9
10
11
12
13
14
15
16
17
18
19
20
21
22

Training plan

Training

Overview
- Describe which role Training will play in addressing the priority barriers for change
- Describe the process and collaboration partners in planning and executing Training

Details

Key levers	Purpose of channel	Receivers
Class room		
Video		
Skype		
Operating procedures		
Learning email		
Others (describe)		

Change plan

Based on the last 2 documents, you can create your change plan. This is geared toward 3 areas: Organizational changes, Change relay inside the organization and communication. The last one is based on a more detailed document that precisely described each communication venue and channel.

Communication

Overview
- Describe which role communication will play in addressing the priority barriers for change
- Describe the process and collaboration partners in planning and executing communication

Details

Key levers	Purpose of channel	Receivers
Mass communication		
Targeted communication		
Campaigns		
1-1 communication		
Others (describe)		

3

Organization design

Overview
- Describe how organisation design will address the priority barriers for change
- Describe the process and collaboration partners in planning and executing organisational design changes

Details

Key levers	Description of change	Receivers of org. change
New or existing KPIs		
Change organisational units/functions		
Headcounts (reduction/addition)		
Role descriptions/ reporting lines		
Other (describe)		

Role in change cascading

Overview

- Describe which which business roles will play in addressing the priority barriers for change
- Describe the process and collaboration partners in planning and the work of the business roles

Details

Type of business roles	Purpose of involvement	Participants (to extend possible)
User group (if necessary)		
Relay inside the organization		
Super users		
Senior stakeholders		
Other (describe)		

3

191

CHANGE MANAGEMENT COMMUNICATIONS PLAN

PROJECT NAME		DATE CREATED	
PROJECT MGR.		VERSION DATE	
ORGANIZATION		VERSION NO.	

Identify affected stakeholders and describe required communication.

EVENT / ACTION / STRATEGY	PROJECT PHASE(S)	EST. DATE OF EFFECT	TARGETED STAKEHOLDERS	REASON FOR COMMUNICATION	METHOD OF COMMUNICATION
Announcement of Change	1.5	14-Jan			
Change Implementation Training	2.3, 2.4.1, 2.5, 2.6	19-Jan			
Activity 1		Jan-Feb			
Activity 2		Feb			

Readiness survey

The Need for Change	Strongly disagree	Disagree	Neutral	Agree	Strongly agree
This organization needs to change					
I know what the vision for the change looks like					
I am aware of the reasons why change is needed					
There are a number of good, rational reasons for this change to be made					
The scope of the proposed change is appropriate and achievable					

Leadership and Management

	Strongly disagree	Disagree	Neutral	Agree	Strongly agree
The senior managers are committed to the change					
There is visible leadership of the change by the managers					
The managers will support the staff during the change					
I have the opportunity to discuss the change with my line manager					

Attitude to Change

		Strongly disagree	Disagree	Neutral	Agree	Strongly agree
I think that the change will be beneficial for me						
I believe that the change will benefit the organisation						

Communications

				Strongly disagree	Disagree	Neutral	Agree	Strongly agree
The communications I have received so far about the change have been useful								
The communications I have received so far about the change have been well-timed								
I understand how I can provide feedback on the change								
I think there is enough consultation with staff on the changes								

Preparation for Change

		Strongly disagree	Disagree	Neutral	Agree	Strongly agree
I feel that I have the necessary skills and knowledge to make this change work						
I think that change is usually well-planned in the organisation						
The organisation usually provides appropriate training for those who need it						
The staff at the organization generally have the skills required for this change and will be able to build on these						

196

Benefit realization

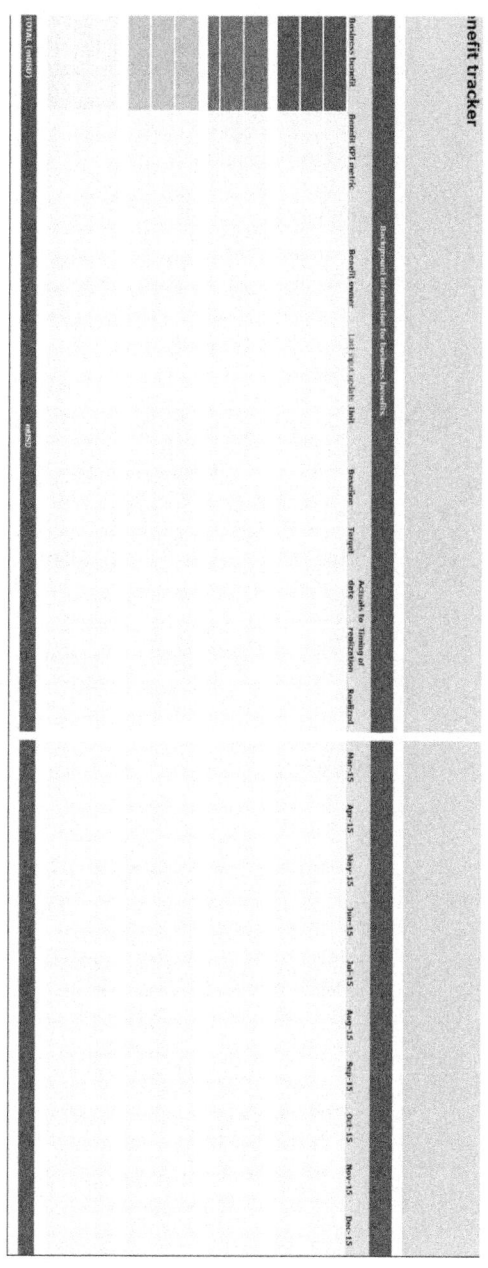

REFERENCES

1. https://www.prosci.com/change-management/what-is-change-management

2. Filicetti, John (August 20, 2007). Project Management Dictionary". PM Hut.

3. Conner, Darryl, (1992). Managing at the speed of change

4. Conner, Daryl (August 15, 2012). The Real Story of the Burning Platform".

5. Phillips Julien (1982) Human Resource Management

6. Beckhard, Richard Harris, Rubin (1977) Organizational Transitions: Managing Complex Change

ADDITIONAL NOTES

In a true agile fashion, as the Product Owner (and Scrum Master and Development Team) of this book, I will continuously correct it, improve it and add to its content. If you have any feedback, please contact me at the following email address: okazandj@hotmail.com. If you bought the first version, you an also contact me at this address and I will end you the extension in pdf format.

Printed in Great Britain
by Amazon